sign language interpreting:
a basic resource book

SHARON NEUMANN SOLOW

ILLUSTRATIONS BY
FRANK ALLEN PAUL

A PUBLICATION OF
THE NATIONAL ASSOCIATION OF THE DEAF
814 Thayer Avenue
Silver Spring, Maryland 20910

© 1981 by Sharon Neumann Solow
Softcover
ISBN: 0-913072-44-3
Hardcover
ISBN: 0-913072-45-1
Eighth Printing, 1992
Ninth Printing, 1993
Tenth Printing, 1994
Eleventh Printing, 1996
Twelfth Printing, 1996
Thirteenth Printing, 1997

Acknowledgements

I wish to express my gratitude to Virginia Hughes; she "taught me everything I know."

I also wish to express my gratitude to Dr. Ray L. Jones and the National Center on Deafness for the tremendous support and assistance rendered by its personnel in the preparation of this book.

I wish to also thank Arlene Benson for her wonderful assistance in editing the manuscript, Barbara Reade who helped me to develop the concept of this book, John Kralick for his endeavors in compiling the bibliography, Mel Carter, Jr. for all of his assistance in publication, and Marina McIntire for helping immeasurably in the completion of this work.

My deepest gratitude goes to my parents, Don and Hertha Neumann who gave me the language and the desire to enter this field.

Finally, I thank Larry Solow for his assistance in clarifying my thinking and for his support both personally and professionally.

PROLOGUE

The field of interpreter training is beginning to come of age. It may be true that we cannot teach signers to be interpreters, but it is certainly true that many signers can learn to be interpreters. Ms. Neumann Solow has written a book that will facilitate learning the art of sign language interpreting. For the student it presents the important issues and expertise which must be mastered. For the teacher it presents an excellently arranged guide. Interpreter training has suffered for lack of adequate materials. This book will help end that dearth, and stimulate our work to greater success.

Louie J. Fant, Jr.

This is a timely document. Federal and state mandates have made sign language interpreters an integral part in the assimilation of deaf citizens into the mainstream of American society. Accordingly, the preparation of interpreters calls for the development of publications and materials that will provide them appropriate skills and techniques.

Sharon Neumann Solow's thoroughly researched and comprehensive book not only promises to be a significant and useful contribution to the field of interpreter training, but also indicates that sign language interpreting is rapidly maturing as a profession.

The National Center on Deafness has been deeply involved in interpreter training since 1964, when it initiated its first formal interpreter training coursework. This publication also underscores the Center's continuing commitment to build sign language and interpreting to reach full maturity, with the promise that this holds for the deaf community throughout the United States.

Ray L. Jones, Ed.D.
Director, National Center on Deafness
California State University, Northridge

Table of Contents

Introduction

The room settles, the speaker finds her position, clears her throat and begins. A few milliseconds behind the speaker, a pair of hands reaches up and begins to form sentences in the air. These hands belong to a sign language interpreter, who is taking the thoughts, words, emotions, and nuances of the speaker and putting them into a visual form of communication.

The second speaker finds his position. He is a leader in his community and argues strongly and articulately for the rights of all people to live full and happy lives. This man stretches out his hands and begins. A few milliseconds later a voice is heard. This voice belongs to a sign language interpreter, who is transmitting the thoughts, words, emotions and nuances of the signer into an auditory form.

The sign language interpreter acts as a communication link between people, serving only in that capacity. An analogy is in the use of a telephone — the telephone is a link between two people that does not exert a personal influence on either. It does, however, influence the ease of communication and the speed of that process. If the interpreter can strive to maintain that parallel positive function without losing vital human attributes, then the interpreter renders a professional service.

Throughout the day, every situation involving communication holds potential for the use of a sign language interpreter. Many activities that hearing people in the United States take for granted might be a source of great effort for a person with hearing impairment. Take, for example, the simple cancellation of an appointment. A hearing-impaired person needs to have access to a telecommunication device (which transmits typed messages over the phone,) and the person that he or she had the appointment with would also need to have access to one. If the person being contacted does not have such a device, then the deaf person might have to drive over to cancel, or rely on a hearing friend to call and cancel. Ideally, the deaf person would have access to the service of a sign language interpreter to enable him or her to directly make contact.

Casual daily encounters with people are often marked by deceptively simple communication that is often taken for granted. In a store, think of the ease with which communication occurs between hearing persons. One automatically and without effort says, "excuse me" on the street when bumping into people. When one's back is turned, it is normal to hear a friend calling out and to then be able to respond. A hearing person, without even trying, can tune in to a nearby conversation or one side of a telephone conversation, sometimes not even remembering where that little tidbit of information was picked up. All of these and more are the luxuries of having hearing that functions well.

The challenge for sign language interpreters is the equalization of communication for hearing and hearing-impaired people. Interaction between hearing and hearing-impaired individuals may present particular challenges because there are other things to consider beyond mere language differences. While it is often true that these people do not share the same language, it may also be the case that these individuals do not share the same culture. As interpreters, we must function in a very real way as the ears of one person and the eyes of the other. Beyond this, we must serve as cultural bridges as well.

The situation of the sign language interpreter is unique in many ways. When two hearing persons from different countries try to communicate, both parties involved can hear. The foreign language interpreter is not required to pass on auditory information so much as to translate the words and inflections of speakers. By contrast, a sign language interpreter serves as a complete auditory link to the deaf person, who relies on the interpreter to know, for example, that an airplane is passing overhead, or that a sudden rainfall has caused the others in the room to look out the window.

As first-class citizenship becomes more and more of a reality for all people, increasing attention is being given to the special ways in which we can offer everyone an equal opportunity to participate in the events of the world. The new catchwords are "equal access," including equal access to information. Interpreters can play an important role in this process of equalization by making information and people accessible. In order to live up to this challenge, we must strive to develop the necessary skills to best provide this access to the populations that rely on us to transmit information between them.

The skills required of a sign language interpreter start, naturally, with language competency. Interpreters must be fluent in both languages they use. In our case the two languages are English and American Sign Language, or whatever sign system is being used. (Different systems of manual communication will be discussed in depth in Chapter 2.) Beyond language capability, the interpreter needs some other very subtle skills. As mentioned earlier, the task is not only transmitting from one language to another, but also involves the inclusion of peripheral sounds and other modifications that apply to communication when a deaf person is involved.

Our profession is relatively new and operates with little or no external regulation. Therefore, a portion of the task involves the interpreter using judgment to deal with various situations. That judgment must be a form of self-regulation for the interpreter and for the entire field, which in turn will influence the behavior and underlying attitudes of sign language interpreters. The basis for judgment must be reliable information and a solid philosophical foundation. A fundamental goal of this book is to provide some of that information for people new to the field and those who seek a higher level of sophistication in the area of sign language interpreting.

Definition of Terms

As in any specialized area of endeavor, sign language interpreting has its unique vocabulary.

Interpreting

1. INTERPRETING
    The process of transmitting spoken English into American Sign Language and/or gestures for communication between deaf and hearing people.[1]

2. TRANSLITERATING
   The process of transmitting spoken English into any one of several English-related or English-oriented varieties of manual communication for communication between deaf and hearing people.

In this book the term "interpreting" is often used generically to refer to interpreting and transliterating, as defined above. *Transliterating* will mean specifically staying within one language, but changing modes. Notice the crucial distinction between *transliterating* and *interpreting;* only the latter involves the use of two separate languages. (See Chapter 2.)

3. SIGN-TO-VOICE INTERPRETING

   The process of transmitting American Sign Language or gestured communication into spoken English for communication between hearing and deaf people.

4. SIGN-TO-VOICE TRANSLITERATION

   The process of transmitting English-related or English-oriented varieties of manual communication into spoken English for communication between hearing and deaf people.

Once again, Sign-to-Voice or Voice "Interpreting" is the generic term applied to both tasks.[2]

Visual Communication

1. AMERICAN SIGN LANGUAGE[3]
   The language of the deaf community. It is a language in and of itself with a syntax and vocabulary different from English. Also known as *ASL, Ameslan,*[4] *the sign language of deaf people* or *Sign Language.*

2. PIDGIN SIGN ENGLISH
   A variety of manual communication in which characteristics of both English and ASL are combined. Also referred to as *PSE, Siglish, Sign English, manual English, or Signed English.*

3. MANUAL ALPHABET

   The process of expressing the letters of the English alphabet on the hand. It directly represents the English spelling system. Also known as *Fingerspelling* or *Dactylology*.

4. INITIALIZED SIGNS

   Signs that represent English words but are based on traditional signs. Traditional signs are adapted to incorporate the handshape of generally the first letter of the English word desired. The base sign is chosen because it has a similar meaning or conceptual relationship with the English word.[5]

5. MANUAL COMMUNICATION

   The generic term for any communication using signs and/or fingerspelling. This is also known as *sign language* or *signs*.

6. PANTOMIME

   A nonverbal form of communication which is not bound to a certain group of people who speak the same language. It is the freer gestural system of communication which crosses the boundaries of language. Pantomime is the way many deaf people get across some of the ideas they are trying to share when they are communicating with non-signing people or with foreign individuals. This will be discussed in depth in Chapters 2 and 8.

Deafness

1. DEAFNESS

   Since we are mostly dealing with deaf people from a social or lay point of view, I will use Davis and Silverman's social criterion for deafness. They define deafness as existing when "everyday auditory communication is impossible or very nearly so."[6] The term deaf will be used generically in this book. Also known as *Hearing Impaired or Hearing Handicapped*.

2. HARD-OF-HEARING

   Theoretically can describe a person whose hearing ranges between normal and inability to hear (deaf), and ranges from someone who simply requires the other person to talk louder, to the person who hears but cannot make out words. A person who may be audiologically deaf may hear some environmental sounds and might also fall into this category. In either case a loss of sensitivity in the ear or of its nerves is involved.

3. MINIMAL LANGUAGE COMPETENCY
   Used to refer to those deaf individuals with little or no education, and whose command of ASL and English is either poor or nonexistent. Also known as *MLC, Minimal Language Skills, MLS, Minimal Communication Skills, or, MCS*[7]. (See Chapter 8.)

The Field of Interpreting

Interpreting is a challenging field with some very unique qualities that set it apart as a profession. It would be difficult to find another field that offers such a variety of experiences. Interpreters serve in nearly every kind of classroom, medical setting, service situation, or therapy setting that occurs, and this list could be expanded indefinitely. To put it simply, an interpreter can be exposed to whole worlds of information and thrust into situations demanding professional preparation or training.

Historically, the interpreter was a person who worked with deaf people in some other capacity or who just happened to know sign language. There was no such thing as a *professional* interpreter. These people were the pioneers of the field as we know it today. Most of them volunteered long hours and, through their generosity, helped train the next generation of interpreters. Now things have changed to the point that interpreters are hired in many situations and are paid for their services. No longer must deaf people feel obligated to a kind person who donated hours of her or his personal time to help. Now a deaf person can expect, without excessive gratitude, a professional to handle the situation and to handle it well.

Historically there was also virtually no training for people who wished to become sign language interpreters. Now there are several institutions which train interpreters to work in formal and informal settings. More and more information about sign language interpreting and the interrelationship of the experiences of the deaf and hearing people is being shared and taught.

This growth can only bode well for the deaf and hearing people served by the interpreting profession. Interpreting service can be obtained from professionals who are prepared to render this service in a variety of ways.

---

[1]TRANSLATING in *Interpreting for Deaf People* was historically what is now transliterating. Translating, in common usage, is usually considered equivalent to the term *Interpreting;* however, it is specifically used in reference to the written task, with more preparation time.

[2]Sign-to-voice interpreting/transliterating was historically called "reverse interpreting". This term is no longer in favor among professionals, but as in any area, terminology takes time to change.

[3]Hereafter referred to as ASL.

[4]The acronym, Ameslan, was coined by Louie J. Fant, Jr. (1972).

[5]There are some unique cases of old initialized signs, such as WINE, IDEA, and KING, which have no base sign with a different handshape.

[6]Davis, Hallowell and Silverman, S. Richard; *Hearing and Deafness,* Fourth Edition, Holt, Rinehart & Winston, NY 1978, p. 88.

[7]The term "low verbal" is obsolete due to its negative connotations.

Chapter 1

Interpreter Role and Behavior

The Function of an Interpreter

The service an interpreter provides can be summed up as follows: interpreters attempt to equalize a communication-related situation so that the deaf and hearing participants involved have access to much the same input and output or can take advantage of the same resources. While sign language interpreters generally pass on the vocalized English equivalents of signed information, it is also necessary that they transmit all significant auditory input into visual form. There is more to an interpreter's job than merely transmitting the signed equivalents of words that are heard.

Actions and incidents may be puzzling to a deaf person unless environmental clues are transmitted by the interpreter. For example, the reason that everyone in class turned their heads may have been because someone in the back of the room was coughing, or because a jet flying overhead had cut off the sound of the voices in the room. An interpreter explaining that a speaker has a very strong accent, that a clock is ticking very loudly, that the others in the room are very silent, and so on is "tuning in" the deaf person to various environmental clues. For example, a class was intently working on a difficult mathematical theorem when it suddenly began to rain. All the hearing students turned their heads to look out the window. The interpreter pointed out that the rain had begun falling so suddenly and loudly that it had startled everyone. The deaf student was surprised to learn that rain could make noise, and was able to understand such comments as, "Oh, I've no umbrella!"

Though pointing out environmental sounds is desirable, it would be impossible to transmit everything we physically hear, such as the regular ticking of the clock, or the sound of the wind or an occasional cough in the room. We will constantly find ourselves returning to the term, *judgment.* Sooner or later, most professionals realize that their own sense of what is appropriate may be relied upon fairly heavily throughout their careers. This is also true of the sign language interpreter. Since we work with people and not things, there will always be intangible factors with which to deal. The interpreter must determine the relevance of a certain bit of auditory input within a given situation and then quickly decide whether or not to transmit that bit of information. There is, of course, no choice as to the information presented by a speaker, which the interpreter will always faithfully transmit. However, sometimes there is simply not enough time to transmit all extraneous information, such as the accent or the lisp of a peer, or the sound of cars passing. This kind of information will necessarily take a back seat to the main information being transmitted.

Sign language interpreting is generally done *simultaneously,* meaning that the interpreter is signing or voicing while the originator of the message is talking or signing. This is considered possible because we do not interpret into the same mode as the originator's. We are silently communicating while the speaker is audibly talking or vice versa. It is relatively easy to simultaneously transliterate into Signed English, since it is then not necessary to alter the grammar; however, it is very difficult to do simultaneous interpreting (i.e., into ASL), as this requires syntax changes, and more reliance on the interpreter's memory.

Qualities of Interpreters

The characteristics of a professional interpreter are many, and after a while the list begins to look like the Girl Scout Code or the Golden Rule. Interpreter behavior refers to actions while interpreting; however, there is no attempt to reform those who enter the field to become better or different people. Interpreters have a right to their individuality, but there are many qualities that can help to clarify the role and functioning of a professional sign language interpreter.

Interpreting requires flexibility. Interpreters are constantly bombarded with new words, both in English and in ASL, and must be flexible enough to incorporate what is learned into their own systems. Flexibility is necessary in order for an interpreter to fit into any situation. Since interpreters are the vehicles for communication between many kinds of people, they should be prepared to fit into the various situations in which they find themselves. Interpreters conceivably can be used in any situation.

Interpreters have worked in situations ranging from athletic events to zoology classes. Interpreters have been used at religious ceremonies that are new to them and very different from those of their own religion. Interpreters have responded to strictly oral situations, such as the interpreter who was asked to lipread to re-construct the sound track of a film, the script of which had been lost and there are interpreters who never rely on the oral mode. Sometimes an interpreter transmits from one silent mode into another while another interpreter then passes on the information to the hearing members of the group. In this instance there are two interpreters and only one who speaks.

Interpreters have even been used to help researchers understand the signs used by chimpanzees. During a single day an interpreter may be asked to interpret for a sports event and then for a very formal awards banquet. In that same day one consumer may prefer to use ASL while the next consumer will rely heavily on lipreading, and a third consumer may request fingerspelling in addition to signs. *Flexibility* will help the interpreter fit into these different situations.

Objectivity is an essential quality of a professional interpreter. This quality requires the skill of showing no favoritism and of not revealing one's own feelings while interpreting. The interpreter typically cares deeply about the welfare of the individuals being served, but must maintain a form of "detached involvement," caring about the people involved without investing feelings in the situation. If the interpreter becomes involved in an interpreting situation, it is quite possible that it could influence the interpretation; this in turn could affect the situation. By remembering the basic principle of the interpreter as facilitator only, it is possible to be objective so as to do an effective job.

Self-discipline is a quality that probably is the basis for most of the more specific items mentioned. Because interpreters work basically alone, with little or no supervision, interpreting is not an easy profession to monitor. It is nearly impossible to supervise the work of an interpreter. Often the parties involved are either signers who are deaf or speakers who are hearing, and typically the reason the interpreter is present at all is that there is no one else present who has bimodal or bilingual skills. Therefore, neither communicator in such a situation is in an appropriate position to evaluate the effectiveness and honesty of the interpreter. It is thus the responsibility of the interpreter to set his/her own limits. The interpreter cannot be the sort of person who waits for others to enforce the rules, but rather must have an intrinsic set of values.

Self-discipline evidences itself in the interpreter who turns down an interpreting task that is not appropriate for him or her to handle. It is also self-discipline that helps the interpreter to stifle his or her reactions and thus avoid influencing the people involved in the situation. Interjecting one's own feelings into a particular setting would be truly stepping out of the role of an interpreter; yet without self-discipline, it would be quite difficult to prevent certain strong emotions from showing.

The actions of interpreters reflect on each other, as well as on the interpreting profession as a whole. An attitude of professionalism is a characteristic that every profession needs in order to maintain the kind of standards that go along with being a professional. Self-policing is one function of the profession, as most professionals operate with little or no real supervision. As professionals, we are responsible for our personal growth, as well as for the growth of our profession.

Skill in both target modes, spoken and signed, is necessary, along with the ability to "meet the need" by being fluent in whatever is required so that the most appropriate system can be used for each occasion. This necessitates an ability to assess the communication needs of the individuals relying on the interpreter for service. We often focus our efforts on building our sign skills and vocabulary; however, it is also essential to build our English vocabulary and skills. It cannot be overly stressed that an interpreter needs skill in both languages — not just one — in order to function properly.

The interpreter needs to be sensitive to the unique position she or he is in, the third and often unwanted party. "Unwanted" means that very often consumers of interpreter services must allow a stranger to know some very intimate details of their lives, and this must sometimes be difficult, even with the knowledge that the information will go no further.

It is difficult enough for a person to share private information with a person such as a social worker, doctor or lawyer, who by virtue of his or her profession is privileged to know. Think how much more uncomfortable it must be to have to reveal this information in front of a third person, no matter how vital that person might be to the process.

The interpreter must strive at all times to maintain a low profile, so that the attention of the participants is not focused on him or her. Notice that there are times when this can be taken to unnecessary extremes, as for example, the time that an interpreter almost passed out from an allergic reaction to cigarette smoke rather than interrupt the class she was interpreting to ask a man to put out his cigarette.

On one occasion, an interpreter was in a mental hospital interpreting in a group therapy session. Across the room was a deaf person, and the interpreter was seated in the circle of people. One patient next to the interpreter kept asking why her hands were shaking. The therapist said all the right things, that the interpreter's hands were not shaking, that rather she was signing. But the patient could not seem to comprehend this and kept on mumbling to the interpreter that it would be all right, not to worry, and that lots of people are frightened at first in a mental hospital. Finally he held the hands of the interpreter, trying to "calm" her. These are unusual situations and require tact and careful handling.

Punctuality and responsibility cannot be stressed too much. It is essential to the entire experience that the interpreter arrive on time so that the communication, which the interpreter provides, can proceed. Obviously, the interpreter is only useful while on the job, and absence removes the deaf and hearing person's bridge for communication.

On the other hand, it is important to remember that one problem that plagues many service professions is the misconception that the provider of the service can never be absent. This simply is not true. However, it is crucial to arrange either for a substitute interpreter or a change of date or time. An ill or inattentive interpreter would probably put in a less-than-effective appearance. This might be worse than an absence, since hampered performance could cause misunderstanding.

The sign language interpreter acts as a link between hearing and deaf persons. Again, the analogy is in the use of a telephone as a link between two people that does not exert a personal influence on either. The interpreter strives for a parallel positive function without losing one's humanness. If this is maintained, the interpreter-client relationship will be on much firmer ground.

It is important to keep in mind that the satisfaction derived from an interpeter's work should stem from a sense of a *communication* job well done and not necessarily the repercussions to the client at some other level. To illustrate this point, an educational interpreter could consider the student's final grade a direct evaluation of his or her skill as an interpreter. That interpreter would, in effect, be taking any credit or blame away from the participants in the class, the teacher and the student. Other problems that might result from this attitude might be a great deal of patronizing behavior toward the deaf student, checking on progress, and other displays of concern over the student's performance in the class. An example of patronization can be in the overly "helpful" person who indicates a lack of faith in the client.

There is also the possibility of a false sense of success or failure in the interpreter. It is conceivable that an excellent interpreter might interpret for a failing student, and a minimally skilled interpreter could interpret for a highly successful student. This is a point that might help us remember where our influence lies. We must value our skills in the area of seeing the client's needs and doing our best to meet those needs in the communications sphere, such as picking the appropriate sign system and physical setting and establishing a comfortable, nonthreatening atmosphere.

Thought Questions

1. What is the basic function of an interpreter?
2. List five qualities of a good interpreter and discuss their importance. Give examples where they might affect a situation.
3. What are some appropriate bases for a sense of success or failure as an interpreter?
4. How could the interpreter transmit the concept of a constant clicking in the radiator?
5. Under what circumstances might the interpreter decide to transmit that information? Under what conditions might she or he decide not to transmit it?

Chapter 2

Sign Systems and Situation Assessment

Sign Systems

Sign language is a generic term for many forms of manual communication. Many systems of sign English have been developed in response to a desire on the part of some educators who saw a need for a method to teach English to deaf children. Many of these English sign systems currently in use are the center of a great deal of controversy from linguistic and educational standpoints. As interpreters, we need not concentrate on the controversy at this point; however, for our own use and understanding, it is important to know what is happening.

There are two *languages* among the various systems outlined on the chart in this section (p. 12). These two languages are English and ASL. All others are *systems of communication;* some are naturally occurring and some are contrived; most are based on both of the languages.

Terms

ASL

American Sign Language, the language typically used among deaf adults. A language in and of itself, with its own grammar

9

and vocabulary. There is minimal use of fingerspelling in ASL. ASL is different from English and has a genetic relationship to French Sign Language.[1]

Pidgin Sign English (PSE)

The generic term for naturally occurring varieties which incorporate traditional ASL signs, some newer and contrived signs, and fingerspelling in flexible grammatical order. Popular nomenclature for PSE includes Sign English, Signed English, Siglish, CASE, and Ameslish. Although CASE and Ameslish are distant from one another, they fit within the same category of the continuum.

Conceptually Accurate Signed English (CASE): The communication style characterized by the incorporation of traditional ASL signs, some newer signs, some contrived signs and fingerspelling, along with speech and speechreading, signed in English grammatical order to represent English visually. Signs are organized in English order with minimal changes, and English is mouthed exactly as spoken in the original English that is interpreted. Signs are used with an attempt to retain the meaning from ASL rather than English, so that "right" would be signed different ways depending on its meaning.

Ameslish: A term applied differently by different people. For use in this book, Ameslish will refer to ASL signing with minimal incorporation of English, more fingerspelling than is typically used in ASL, and some deviation from ASL idiomatic use.

Manually Coded English

The generic term for contrived systems for encoding English in manual form. These systems of visual English are attempts to precisely represent the English language, both its grammar and vocabulary, through the means of speech and speech reading, and the use of a combination of traditional signs, newer signs, contrived signs and fingerspelling. Contrived signs are generally based to some degree on ASL signs. Signs are usually selected on a "one sign one word" basis, deviating in some significant ways from the meaning of the original ASL signs. Sound and spelling are generally the deciding factors in sign selection, rather than meaning. Thus, all meanings of the word "right" would be signed the same, while "write" would be signed differently. Signs are placed in English order with signs to represent English grammatical forms, such as suffixes and prefixes. MCE was devised as a means of teaching English to youngsters. Examples of MCE are SEE[1][2], SEE[2][3], LOVE[4], Manual English[5], and Signed English[6].

Rochester Method
The communication systems utilizing fingerspelling, speech and speechreading to represent English manually.

Cued Speech
A system of organized gestures used to aid in lipreading. These gestures are used to distinguish between sounds that look alike on the lips, such as /b/, /p/, and /m/.[7]

Oral Method
The communication system that incorporates speech and speechreading only; no signs or gestures are involved in the oral method. This refers also to an educational philosophy emphasizing the exclusive use of speech and speechreading.

English
The language spoken, written and read by the majority of people in the United States, England and several other countries of the world.

Reader's Theater
A technique for presenting poetry, prose and plays using a certain amount of dramatic technique such as pantomime.

Pantomime
A more universal method of communication through gestures; a nonverbal system of communication.

Narrative Style
A form of ASL storytelling style, incorporating techniques from pantomime.

Pantomine is included in the sign systems chart because it plays a large part in the communication modes of and with deaf people. First of all, pantomime is the sole communication mode used by some deaf people, such as those with minimal language competency (see Chapter 8). It is also the mode many deaf individuals use with people who do not know how to sign. Pantomime also enters the picture in *narrative style* in that storytell-

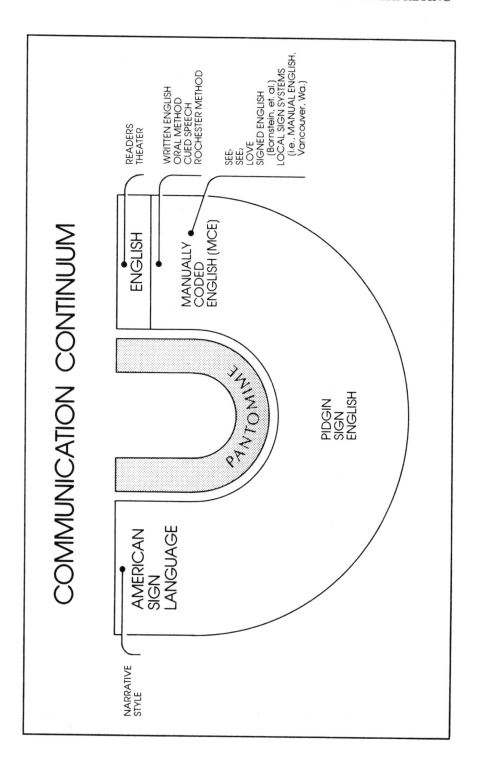

ers rely heavily on pantomime to provide interest and drama to signed stories. An analogous situation is *Reader's Theater,* which combines pantomime with speech for dramatic effect.

As interpreters, we should be aware of pantomime so that we can incorporate pantomime techniques to make our communication—both our signing and our reading of signing—more effective and clear. Techniques we can borrow from pantomime include such things as characterization, handling of objects appropriately, and representation of emotions facially and physically. Pantomime, however, is not sign language and sign language is not pantomime. Many people make the error of confusing the two, perhaps because they are both visual; however, one is a language and the other is a means of communication, not a language.

Manually Coded English (MCE) is often referred to as the SEE systems after SEE_1 and SEE_2. These are sign systems that have been contrived within the last decade for educational purposes. SEE_1, SEE_2 and LOVE all started out as a single system, but because of differences in approach, branched out into three separate systems. They still share many characteristics and basic tenets. Although many of the signs are based on the traditional signs from ASL, these signs are not used in the same grammatical, syntactic or semantic sense as in ASL. For example, there are at least three signs in ASL which denote the various meanings of the English word "right," while a single sign represents this word in any Manually Coded English system.

Many of the systems on the chart are attempts to make English visible on the hands and/or mouth. Most of the visualized English systems were designed for use in the education of deaf children. As interpreters, we must remember that our task is not the improvement of deaf people's language (ASL or English), but rather communication between individuals. Sometimes a particular program will require the use of English or one of the systems of visualized English. In these cases, it is the responsibility of the interpreter to transmit into and from that specified system.

Situation Assessment

On the whole, there are several assumptions that the sign language interpreter can make in determining the mode of communication to use with each deaf audience he or she approaches. Every audience will require certain modifications in style, vocabulary and sign system to meet its unique needs. The skill of the interpreter rests in part on his or her ability to make the appropriate decisions regarding these choices. Probably the best and easiest way to determine the appropriate sign system is to ask the deaf persons in the audience themselves or to ask the organizers if they are aware of the deaf members' preferences as a whole. A danger here is that not all people, even those heavily involved with deafness, are fully aware of the different sign systems and communication styles used among deaf people. Therefore, it is often up to the interpreter to make this determination on his or her own.

It is important to remember that any suggestions on choice of approach to communication in this section are based on assumptions and that every individual situation will have to be weighed for appropriate selection.

For most mixed and/or large audiences, such as mass media viewers, or people attending religious services or a public forum, the interpreter would most probably lean toward ASL as the primary mode of communication, since the largest number of deaf persons would be served by that choice. Again, it is important to check with the people in the audience, if at all feasible, in order to learn their own preference as to sign system. It is well to be aware that some deaf people are highly offended by the assumption that they will prefer an ASL interpretation and feel rightly or wrongly that it is an insult to their intelligence. This is likely a result of years of propaganda that ASL is somehow lower in status than English. Years of being told one uses "bad language" is very difficult to erase. This point is made with the intention of sensitizing the interpreter, and is not intended as any form of value judgment. Where the audience is mixed, invariably there is the need for careful determination of a middle ground within the audience and to adjust the communication accordingly. Many people who can understand and use various forms of signed English can also understand ASL, regardless of their preference. These people are willing to sacrifice a desire for English for the sake of understanding and participation by the majority of the members of the audience with the use of ASL or Ameslish.

Pidgin Signed English (PSE), in whichever form seems appropriate, would fit the general needs of an academic classroom or professional conference, or a college or university. Many high schools and other educational institutions hire interpreters with the specific requirement that they use a particular style or system of MCE. The use of one of these specified systems would then be typically considered part of the contract, and to accept such a job, the interpreter must be prepared to follow the policy of the hiring institution.

Pantomime, in combination with some very rudimentary and simple signing, is used for communication with deaf individuals with minimal language competency. This area of interpreting requires some very special and sophisticated skills. Unlike Sign English interpreting, interpreting for deaf people with minimal language competency requires time to stop and check for understanding, and time to get continuous feedback. The ability to both use and understand pantomimic communication is essential in this mode of communication. For those further interested in this area of interpreting, minimum language competency interpreting will be discussed at greater length in a later chapter.

If asking the clients involved which system they prefer the interpreter to use does not succeed, then the interpreter might consider observing conversation among deaf clients before the interpreting assignment, or conversing with the client or clients, to determine the sign system that seems most comfortable for them. Such a decision carries a certain liability in that the clients might see the interpreter in the light of a primary interactor rather than a communication bridge that is not directly involved. It is also possible that an unsophisticated client might try to talk through the upcoming situation with the interpreter, which again places the interpreter in the role of a primary interactor. This kind of conversation should be avoided. With careful handling, the interpreter can maintain a comfortable level of involvement with the clients.

Finally, there is another way to determine the best system to use while interpreting—the technique of reading one's audience. This means reading the body language and other nonverbal cues for evidence of comfort and/or discomfort with the signing system being used. If a confused or blank expression appears at the incorporation of certain signs, possibly those signs are unfamiliar. If there is a great deal of conversation about certain signs the interpreter is using, perhaps this is a cue that those particular signs or the system from which they derive is unfamiliar. If, on the other hand, deaf clients are constantly asking for the fingerspelled word for signs when initially presented, it may be an indication that they are more English-oriented and might prefer a PSE or MCE version of the presentation.

It is almost always preferable to ask the deaf clients directly involved what their choice of systems might be. If they are not available before the interpreting situation begins, or if they are not able to answer the question due to a lack of sophistication or experience with interpreters, then it is often helpful to check with others who have been involved with the particular situation, such as a previous interpreter or a professional involved. Often, however, situations arise in which the interpreter can get little or no reliable information about the communication methods to be used. In such instances, it is appropriate to rely on the audience's response to the particular vocabulary and communication system chosen, with constant modification as the need arises or becomes evident, including incorporation of signs used by the deaf people in that setting.

Thought Questions

1. What is the function or basic reason for the development of many of the signed English systems?
2. How many true languages are involved in our sign systems? Name them.
3. What system of communication on the systems chart is 'universal'?
4. What system of communication is probably called for in interpreting a television program for a mixed audience?
5. How is pantomime used in verbal communication?
6. How is the determination made as to how to sign certain vocabulary items in SEE_1, SEE_2, and LOVE?
7. What is probably the best way to determine which sign system to use in a given situation? Why?
8. What can the interpreter do while interpreting to assess and meet the communication need within a given situation?

---

[1]Baker, Charlotte and Padden, Carol, *American Sign Language: A Look at Its History, Structure and Community.* Silver Spring, MD. T. J. Publishers, 1978.

Klima, Edward and Bellugi, Ursula. *The Signs of Language.* Cambridge, Mass. Harvard University Press; 1979.

Stokoe, William C.; Croneberg, Carl G.; Casterline, Dorothy C. *A Dictionary of American Sign Language on Linguistic Principles.* (Washington, D.C.) Gallaudet College Press (1976).

[2]Anthony, David, *Seeing Essential English,* University of Northern Colorado, Greeley, CO, 1971.

[3]Gustason, Gerilee; Pfetzing, Donna; and Zawolkow, Esther, *Signing Exact English,* National Association of the Deaf, Silver Spring, MD, 1975.

[4]Wampler, Dennis, *Linguistics of Visual English, Booklets 1-3,* Santa Rosa, CA, 1971.

[3]Gustason, Gerilee; Pfetzing, Donna; and Zawolkow, Esther. *Signing Exact English,* National Association of the Deaf, Silver Spring, MD, 1975.

[6]Bornstein, Harry, *Sign English Dictionary for Preschool and Elementary Levels.* Washington, D.C. Gallaudet College Press, 1975.

[7]Cornett, R. Orin, *Cued Speech and 'Total Communication',* 1978. Model Secondary School for the Deaf.

Chapter 3

Physical Factors and Body Language

Physical Factors

Deaf consumers must be able to see and be seen clearly and hearing consumers must be able to hear and be heard clearly. As interpreters, we need to prepare for and arrange the setting with this in mind.

Since eyes are controlled by muscles and ears are not, receiving communication through the eyes can be more tiring than through the ears. It is important that the interpreter remember this in planning the physical portion of the task.

Position

The interpreter should be close enough to the speaker to make it possible for the deaf consumer to see both the interpreter and the speaker without turning or stretching. At the same time, the interpreter needs to be sensitive to the speaker's sense of space and comfort. Some people feel uncomfortable with the interpreter too near or too far. It is also important to be near enough to the deaf audience so that they are not straining to see. The judgment of the interpreter is essential in determining the physical setup.

Being near the speaker can also aid the interpreter in hearing the speaker more accurately. Since the interpreter cannot look at the speaker directly, proximity is very important. The interpreter cannot rely on lipreading to help distinguish certain sounds, or on gestures that will aid in understanding.

A decision must be made in each situation as to whether the interpreter should sit or stand. When in doubt, the number of deaf people in the audience should be taken into consideration. If there is a large number, it is usually best to stand for the sake of visibility. It is also best to stand during a platform interpreting assignment, or if the audience is any distance from the interpreter. When the speaker moves around a great deal, standing leaves the interpreter in a better position for quick and easy movement.

If the speaker is signing, the voice interpreter should be seated in front of the signer. If a microphone is needed, it should be placed where the voice interpreter is seated. If there are deaf and hearing people presenting and in the audience, then it is wise to have at least two interpreters. One interpreter stands on the platform while the other sits in the audience facing the platform. The responsibility of the interpreter on the platform is to sign the spoken presentation and to vocalize signed comments and questions from the audience. The seated interpreter has the responsibility of voice interpreting the signed presentations and signing to presenters on stage who may be unable to see the platform interpreter. The situation is in actuality much more complex. Anytime an interpreter finds him or herself in such a situation, flexibility, sensitivity and timing will assist in providing thorough service. (See Chapter 7, PLATFORM INTERPRETING.)

Many situations call for different positioning. In a classroom, interpreters generally sit in front of the class, to the side and slightly forward of the teacher unless the deaf person prefers otherwise and as long as interference upon the speaker is not in question. In one-to-one situations, the interpreter and the hearing and deaf consumers generally sit in a triangular formation, with the interpreter facing the deaf consumer and not making eye contact with the hearing consumer. Around a table or in a circle, the interpreter usually sits across from the deaf person(s). In court, the interpreter must be very careful about his or her placement. Interpreters must be audible to the members of the court and, especially, to the court recorder; at other times interpreters will assist in "whispering" between client and lawyer.

Seated or standing, the interpreter needs to check that she or he is in a position where all the deaf people in the audience are able to see the interpreter clearly and where all the hearing people are able to hear. Sometimes it is advisable to have more than one interpreter for a large audience of deaf people, because it can be difficult to read signs from a distance. The problem of reading fingerspelling and lips at a distance is especially great.

If the situation is long or strenuous, one interpreter may not be sufficient to serve the situation. It may be necessary to have two interpreters to spell one another, either by time or by speaker. Some interpreters in this situation take fifteen to thirty-minute turns. Others are assigned to speakers so that the transition is smoother; they simply move to the front at the same time as the speaker.

There are some deaf persons who prefer the interpreter not to be in front of the room. For whatever reason, this preference should be respected. If this is the case, it is certainly the right of the deaf person to make the decision on positioning, as long as there is agreement among all deaf consumers. Obviously, this requires the understanding that the interpreter may not hear what is happening in the classroom or lecture hall.

Positioning is a factor over which we generally have control. Try to find a position before starting the interpreting task so that time and information are not lost while you are trying to get situated. Note interpreter positions in the following illustrations.

1. INTERVIEW

2. CLASSROOM

3. PLATFORM

4. COURTROOM

5. SIGN-TO-VOICE (without microphone)

6. SIGN-TO-VOICE (with microphone)

7. TWO INTERPRETERS

8. AROUND A TABLE

9. IN A CIRCLE

10. LARGE AUDIENCE (several interpreters in various positions)

Background

The background against which an interpreter works is a very important factor that relates to visibility and ease in watching for the deaf person. Background pertains both to the interpreter's clothing and to the background behind the interpreter. Your clothing should offer a plain, solid color that contrasts with your skin. Many interpreters have found the use of an interpreter's smock or jacket (See illustration below.) very useful for several reasons. First of all, the smock helps to provide the necessary background; secondly, it provides a psychological reminder that can be very helpful in maintaining one's role. The use of a jacket helps all parties remember that the interpreter is on the job and should not become involved beyond the role of communication facilitator. The removal of that smock can then permit social interaction before and after the interpreting situation—to whatever degree the individuals involved desire as personal parties. In other words, the smock helps remind people of the interpreter role.

INTERPRETER JACKET

The interpreter should attempt to arrange the physical environment so that he or she signs in front of a contrasting wall or backdrop. A blackboard or divider of appropriate color can make a good background, or one can hang fabric of contrasting color behind the area where the interpreter will be working. In hanging the fabric or backdrop, remember to have it wide enough to frame the interpreter from several angles. A common error is to place the backdrop directly behind the interpreter, with no precautions being taken for deaf viewers not sitting directly in front of the interpreter.

REMOVABLE BACKGROUND FABRIC

CURTAIN

MOVABLE PARTITION

SOLID COLOR WALL

Lighting

Another factor to be considered in the positioning of the interpreter is lighting. It is essential that the interpreter be placed in a location which permits the best possible light on his or her face and hands. There should be no light source behind the interpreter, such as a window, open door or lamp, or from below the interpreter, distorting facial expression. This is also true in the case of the deaf people involved. It is difficult to interpret from sign to voice if the deaf person who is signing is in front of a light source.

Lights can be important in other ways, as for example, in movies when the lights are low or off. On these occasions it is helpful to have a pocket flashlight, which the deaf client holds on the interpreter as the film is being interpreted. Some rooms have dimmer switches or lights which can be set at a comfortably low level for viewing both the movie and the interpreter. If you're caught without a flashlight, or if the batteries are dead, there are some last-minute solutions as well, such as leaving the door slightly ajar to let in a bit of light, using a partially covered overhead projector, a tensor lamp, or an orchestra lamp.

Appearance

There are many little details to be attended to for a truly professional appearance. Hair is off the face; beards and moustaches should be carefully (and honestly) assessed for their possible distraction level. Certainly, facial hair is always trimmed around the lips well enough for ease in speechreading. Makeup is moderate, although many people feel that lipstick is a must for speechreading from any distance, especially in platform situations. Nails are not too long, and natural nail polish can be used, if any is used at all. Glasses should fit well enough so that they do not fly off the face or need constant attention and adjustment. No jewelry is worn that might be noisy or distracting. Gum is never used while on the job.

Clothing

Clothing should be appropriate for the occasion. If the interpreter is planning to interpret in court, it is helpful to know that some judges still require women to wear dresses. By contrast, wearing a dress may be inappropriate for a classroom situation where the interpreter must interpret around machines, such as a welding class. For interpreting during a job interview the interpreter tries to be only an asset and not a liability to the clients involved. If the interpreter is not dressed appropriately, this might lead the employer to believe that the prospective employee does not command respect, or vice versa.

The interpreter dresses conservatively in order to be as unobtrusive as possible and to provide the best possible background for signing. Excessive makeup, noisy or distracting jewelry, and excessive detail in clothing can all be distracting. The basic criteria to use in assessing the appearance of the interpreter is that he or she should be the least obtrusive person in the room and should provide a comfortable, readable background for signing.

Body Language

Because they typically encounter people who do not use their language, deaf people often depend on body language and facial expression to understand their surroundings. Perhaps this knowledge can help interpreters remember to consider these factors in the interpreting process. Since nonverbal information is a primary source of knowledge, interpreters must be sure that they are communicating precisely what is intended through the facial and body modes. A sense of insecurity can turn a statement into a question, for example, if the interpreter has a questioning look when wondering if he or she is signing something correctly.

To carry the true spirit of the speaker, the interpreter must listen carefully to the nonverbal information presented vocally and attempt to convert that information into a visual form; similarly, watch carefully to convert it into a vocal form from a signer. Many of the subtleties of communication, such as sarcasm, jokes, and innuendoes, are on the nonverbal level. We must find effective ways to convey the same nuances through facial and body expression and from the visual form to a voiced form. Many of the techniques of pantomime can be useful in sending nonverbal information. As a general rule, however, we are not pantomiming when we interpret, and pan-

tomime would surely not be subtle enough for a typical interpreting situation. It is a good idea to keep the idea of subtlety in
mind for the purpose of maintaining a low profile as an interpreter, thus remaining unobtrusive. Often people compliment and,
therefore, reinforce interpreters for extreme expressiveness; yet
it might be a higher compliment if there were no comments. This
might imply that the interpretation was so subtle that the client
felt the speaker was signing or speaking for him or herself and
there was no interpreter present.

There are two kinds of expression in interpreting: one is the
emotional aspect of the speaker's tone, which is the one we most
quickly and easily identify, and the other is the expression
which goes along with the grammar of the language. This second
kind of expression is a little more difficult to describe, but includes the expressions that show change of topic, characterization, emphasis of points, questions, statements, or adjectival aspects of nouns and adverbial aspects of verbs, showing degree or
quantity, such as HARD-WORK versus WORK or MANY-
BOATS versus BOAT. These expressions are modified within
the sign or within the utterance without having a separate entity to represent that aspect. This is a property of ASL but can
and should apply to signed English interpreting.

Reading of body language is an important skill of the sign
language interpreter. The interpreter must find ways to express
vocally the visual expression of the deaf person that he or she is
sign-to-voice interpreting. The same rules for transmitting the
spirit of the speaker apply in sign-to-voice interpreting as in
voice-to-sign interpreting. For example, if the signer were to
sign GOOD with a strong movement, the interpreter would vocalize "very good" with a positive inflection in his or her voice.

The interpreter further uses receptive body language skills to
determine to some extent the comprehension of the deaf consumer and whether they are comfortable with the sign system
chosen by the interpreter. One example of a visual indication
that the deaf consumer is not comfortable with the use of new
signs is the mimicking of the new signs with a look of confusion
or a questioning look. If the deaf client does this several times
during the course of an interpretation, the interpreter might
recognize this as a cue to use older or more traditional signs. If,
on the other hand, the deaf client often suggests new signs for
fingerspelled words, or asks for the English equivalent of signs,

this could indicate that this deaf person is interested in translation with an emphasis on English vocabulary rather than ASL vocabulary.

Eye contact is another factor in body language that should concern the interpreter. We need to maintain eye contact with deaf persons for several reasons. With eye contact, the interpreter can tune in to the understanding and preferences of the deaf client. Another reason is that the deaf client can then feel the communication link that eye contact can provide. Notice, however, the interpreter should not have a staring contest with the deaf person, for that will cause discomfort, but should simply maintain general eye contact.

Because sign language is visual, it is essential that we pay attention to our facial and body expression even more than we do to communicating with vocal languages. The deaf person has, in general, highly experienced eyes and will probably receive the signer's body language first and then the speaker's words. We are always communicating visual information, and it is the task of the interpreter to be aware of what is communicated and to try to convey as accurately as possible paralinguistic information, as well as the verbal information that is transmitted through the signs and words chosen.

For an exercise in nonverbal expression, try to sign the same sentence with different emotions and try to speak the same sentence with varied expressions to see how much a change in expression affects the meaning of an utterance. It may be useful to do this in a group and discuss emotions that are difficult to portray. Our faces and our bodies are made up of muscles which, when exercised, can be very well developed and controlled. Once we are sensitive to exactly what they are doing and the effect of their movement in expression, we can control the information we transmit.

Thought Questions

1. Why are visual physical factors important for interpreting?
2. List five aspects of placement that can infuence ease of watching for a deaf person.
3. List three reasons for concern about placement in reference to the interpreter's needs and comfort.
4. Explain the importance of lighting in interpreting.
5. List five aspects of appearance that relate to a professional job of interpreting.
6. Why is dress important for an interpreter? What are some concerns to keep in mind regarding dress in different situations?
7. How do some deaf people use body language other than while signing?
8. What are some subtleties of language that are expressed nonverbally?
9. Why is subtlety important in the interpreter's function as it relates to body language and facial expression?
10. List five verbs and at least five ways they can be modified within the sign to indicate variations in meaning. How can nouns be modified to include extra information? Adjectives? Adverbs?
11. What are the two kinds of expression that an interpreter should be aware of in transmitting information?
12. Why are body language and facial expression important in reading signers?
13. How and why is eye contact important in an interpreting situation?

Chapter 4

Orientation to the Deaf Community

A community is as intangible as a rainbow, yet we all know that such an entity exists. The deaf community is a basic part of the lives of many deaf people. Interpreters need to be familiar with its workings in order to be 1) culturally aware and comfortable, 2) knowledgeable about references made to various aspects of the community, such as acronyms for organizations or name signs for people who are well known in that community, and 3) constantly in a position to upgrade their reading and signing skills and to add new signs and structures to their reading and signing vocabulary. The deaf community is an identifiable force in the world of many deaf and hearing individuals who are involved in that community in any capacity.

As in most closely knit communities, there is a very effective communication system known as the "grapevine." Through this vehicle much information is passed, both rumor and fact. It has often been stated, jokingly, that the inability of most deaf people to use the telephone is no handicap because their communication grapevine is so effective.

The deaf community consists of social units at many levels, from the family to an international organization. There is, at the international level, an organization of deaf people known as the World Federation of the Deaf, which has regular conferences. At the national level there are both professional and nonprofessional organizations of and for deaf people. The National Association of the Deaf (NAD) is an umbrella organization for many other organizations, and is the major voice of deaf people in the United States today. Within the structure of the NAD are state chapters such as the California Association of the Deaf (CAD), and local chapters such as the Metropolitan Washington Association of the Deaf and the Colorado Springs Silent Club. Professional national organizations include the Registry of Interpreters for the Deaf (RID), which has many deaf members, and the Alexander Graham Bell Association, an organization established for those individuals, with a preference for the oral mode.

Publications in the field include *The Deaf American,* a publication of the NAD; the *American Annals of the Deaf,* the official organ of the Conference of Executives of American Schools for the Deaf and the Convention of American Instructors of the Deaf; the *Volta Review,* the publication of the A. G. Bell Association; the *Journal of Rehabilitation of the Deaf,* published by the American Deafness and Rehabilitation Association, and the *Vocational Rehabilitation Journal,* a general periodical in the area of rehabilitation that includes some articles on deafness. There are numerous local publications, such as the newsletters of various religious groups that are organized especially for deaf individuals, or which sponsor programs for deaf people. Also, local organizations and educational programs which have deaf students publish information that can be invaluable for keeping up on the activities of the deaf community.

The Department of Health, Education and Welfare contains a section known as the Deafness and Communicative Disorders Office.[1] Most of us have contact with this broad governmental agency at the local level through the workings of the division known as Vocational Rehabilitation (VR). Often there is a rehabilitation counselor for the deaf (RCD), who specializes in deafness.

Interpreters usually find it advantageous to investigate the various organizations of the deaf community in which they live and to become actively involved, if possible. As is true of any user of any language, it is essential to be associated with the community that uses that language in order to keep current in usage and vocabulary, and to be fully conversant with the cultural aspects of that community.

Like all languages, ASL is alive and changing. This is evidenced by the addition of such vocabulary as ROCKET, which was needed when the space program began, or STREAKING, when that was a fad in the early 1970s. By simply being involved with the deaf community, we are better able to stay abreast of these and many additional changes. Most of us also need a certain amount of practice in the use of ASL, and there is no better way than to maintain contact with deaf people from many walks of life. Community involvement provides this contact.

The education of deaf children is important in understanding the deaf community. Typically the education of deaf people is different in many ways from that of their hearing peers because of their different needs. There are three general types of educational programs for deaf people in this country. The education of deaf children in residential schools differs most significantly from the general education of hearing children. These institutions are usually run by the states in which they are located. Deaf students typically live in dormitories and go to school on the same campus. Often dialectal signs in certain states seem to originate in the residential schools, since historically the majority of signing deaf adults went through residential programs as children. Woodward, 1973[2], has pointed out that long term attendance at a residential school correlates with fluency in ASL. This fact may assist the interpreter in situation assessment (see Chapter 2.) If there is a residential school nearby, it would be helpful to visit the school.

Another type of school program is the day school, which serves deaf students who commute to school daily. As might be expected, these programs tend to exist in larger cities. Day schools vary as to approach; many use Total Communication, usually MCE or PSE, others are oral. A third kind of educational program exists for deaf students in an integrated setting, where both hearing and deaf students attend the same school, which has special classes for deaf students and possibly certain integrated classes, depending on the needs of the particular deaf student. Programs of this last type are referred to as "mainstreaming" programs. Students from such programs may be more accustomed to the use of interpreters and/or may rely on MCE, PSE, or the Oral Method.

Ideally an interpreter can interact with the deaf community in both a formal and an informal manner. An interpreter could become formally involved in governmental and other civic or educational organizations serving or benefitting deaf people. Informally, an interpreter might like to discover where some deaf persons tend to spend their free time, or become involved in a sports activity that has been organized by deaf people. A deaf club in the area would be an interesting place to visit. Some areas have homes for deaf senior citizens, religious programs, and other programs or institutions at which the new person attempting to join the deaf community might be interested in offering service and friendship. Often an interpreter can get a little realistic experience by interpreting for television for deaf people in a group residence, such as dormitory. There is much more in every individual community. The most important thing is to find a productive way to associate with that community, and from the initial contact further contacts will become more readily available.

Thought Questions

1. What are three reasons that it might be beneficial for an interpreter to be aware of the deaf community?
2. What is another term for informal communication among deaf people?
3. Name some of the organizations of deaf people at different levels, both informal and formal.
4. Name three kinds of educational systems for deaf children in the United States.
5. Describe events and ongoing institutions in your local area where deaf people gather. Which of these could you visit?

---

[1]This Department is undergoing changes which may upset its title and organization (1981).

[2]Woodward, J. 1973, Some Observations on Sociolinguistic Variation and American Sign Language. Kansas, *Journal of Sociology,* 9, 2, 191–199.

Chapter 5

The Ethics of Interpreting

Most professions operate under a set of guidelines or a code of ethics. The Ball State Teacher's College Conference in 1964 marks the inception of the Registry of Interpreters for the Deaf (RID). At that conference, the Interpreter's Code of Ethics was established. That this code of ethics has recently undergone some basic revisions is an indication that interpreting is a growing profession (See Appendix A for the complete text).

For many reasons a code of ethics is important to the interpreting profession. First of all, interpreters are in a unique position because they control the flow of information. The interpreter is often the only person in a room who is bimodal/bilingual; therefore, an unscrupulous interpreter could alter what is communicated, with the possibility of going undetected. Thankfully, most interpreters are probably not unscrupulous. There are also people who do not think of themselves as unscrupulous, but function in an unethical manner, perhaps due to a lack of awareness or training. We need a code of ethics to give these possibly well-meaning but unethical individuals a framework for appropriate behavior.

It is essential that interpreters recognize the responsibilities of our profession to adequately protect the rights of deaf and hearing clients, along with our own rights. A code of ethics protects the interpreter and lessens the arbitrariness of his or her decisions by providing guidelines and standards to follow. Sometimes, for example, the deaf or hearing client may ask the interpreter to take on more responsibility than the transfer of information. If the interpreter tells the client that this doesn't seem to be the most effective use of his or her time, or that he or she is not particularly interested in that level of involvement, these responses can cause unnecessary resentment or confusion. The interpreter can rather explain to the clients that it is impossible to comply with a request because it conflicts with the code of ethics of the interpreting profession. When an interpreter acts solely as an individual and must justify every decision on the basis of personal standards, it is easier to falter and end up in an uncomfortable position.

The code of ethics also offers some consistency within the interpreting profession. Through our adherence to the code of ethics, our clients, both hearing and deaf, will know what to expect of us when they call upon us to serve them. This is a critical point; each of us paves the way for the rest who follow. The first interpreter that a person deals with can profoundly affect that person's attitude toward the interpreting profession. If we do a good job of educating clients, the next interpreter's job is then much easier, as the client's expectations are appropriate. Initial contact seems to be a very strong influence on future behavior, so we must always try to be professional and ethical in order to educate the public properly as to our function.

Interpreting ethics involve the equalization of experience for all people involved in a situation. This means that we are aiming for a condition in which the quality of experience is the same whether a person is deaf or hearing.

There are four general principles upon which the code of ethics rests: confidentiality, impartiality, discretion, and professional distance. These will be covered individually below.

Confidentiality

Confidentiality involves the maintenance of privacy of the parties involved in a situation. Breach of confidentiality is the most serious offense an interpreter can commit. Confidentiality is so essential and so basic that, without it, the entire interpreting task might as well not occur. Confidentiality involves trust, and if this trust is lost, many other things are lost as well. If an interpreter cannot be trusted to keep confidences, then that person should not be entrusted with the responsibility of interpreting.

The interpreter is a third party and, regardless of how helpful to the communication process, remains an extra person. The individuals involved would probably prefer to deal with one another directly, removing the third person. Unfortunately an interpreter is often needed, even when it would be preferable for the two persons to communicate directly. If we can imagine how we would feel if we had to speak of intimate matters in the presence of an outside person, we might be just that much more sensitive to our privileged position as interpreters.

As of this writing, the RID is working on a system for enforcement of the code of ethics; but beyond this formal level, if an interpreter breaks confidence, it can easily spread along the "grapevine" and that interpreter's reputation may be ruined in certain circles. On the other hand, the highest form of retribution is the self-respect that is lost by breaking the code of ethics.

Impartiality

Impartiality is another aspect of the code of ethics. The interpreter must remain neutral and not show personal feelings while interpreting. Interpreters cannot allow themselves to show their reactions to situations or to the information they are transmitting. We need to develop a way that we can release our feelings without revealing confidential information and without affecting the situation at hand. Perhaps we can "talk" to a stuffed animal, or beat on a pillow; some people even talk things out in the isolation of their cars on the way home. If we allow our reactions to affect our functioning, we could easily bias the outcome of the event. For example, by interpreting more dramatically for one party than the other in a divorce, we could make that party look better. Without being sensitive to this pitfall, it is possible to do the damage without being fully aware of it.

Impartiality means treating all parties equally. For instance, we must be impartial in eye contact with all deaf clients in a setting. It is easy to maintain eye contact with a very attentive client, but it is rather hard sometimes to keep up eye contact with an equally deserving client who tends to look around or who simply looks less interested.

Interpreters need to treat all clients equally in other aspects as well. It is essential that we avoid siding with or even appearing to side with one client. Sometimes interpreters are asked or are tempted to play the role of advocate for deaf people. As individuals this is fine, even commendable; as interpreters we must keep our role clear. On the job we simply transmit information between clients. Another pitfall is that sometimes interpreters appear to be siding with either the hearing or the deaf client, perhaps because people view other people who share characteristics as "sticking together," i.e., "they're both hearing" or "they both sign." Thus, we must be careful, both in our attitudes and in our behavior. Don't tell one client the other can't follow because he or she is going too fast; don't talk without signing or sign without talking to either client. These are examples of behaviors that could be viewed as indicating prejudice on the part of the interpreter. Simply by being aware of such behaviors and their implications, we can avoid much difficulty.

Sometimes we fall prey to ego and, because we feel it is a reflection on ourselves or our interpreting, are reticent to interpret a "stupid question" and in very subtle ways repress the participation of a student who regularly tends to ask what we view as stupid questions. Another pitfall, in the area of sign-to-voice interpreting, relates to the skill level of the interpreter. Sometimes, when faced with a client who is difficult for that interpreter to vocalize, the interpreter will, in effect, repress that person's participation so as not to be placed in the embarrassing situation of haltingly vocalizing the client. The interpreter must make the atmosphere as comfortable as possible so that everyone will feel free to communicate, to express themselves, or not to express themselves. The interpreter, to the best of his/her ability, must not block communication in any way.

Discretion

Discretion, or the use of judgment, is essential in many aspects of the field of interpreting. An interpreter should be fully aware of his or her own abilities and be willing to turn down an interpreting job if he or she does not feel skilled enough for the specific assignment. In some situations the interpreter may be too personally involved with the individuals in the particular setting. Awareness of one's limitations and the conviction to act upon that awareness is evidence of discretion.

It is often said that "some service is better than no service at all"; however, this can be fallacious in the case of interpreting, for it can be argued that service was rendered symbolically, but not practically. When an interpreter has attempted too difficult an assignment, no one can claim that there was "no service," but for all practical purposes there was no service for the good that service did the deaf and hearing consumers. If the underskilled interpreter passes on erroneous information, it is possible that no one would catch this error; the parties involved could remain ignorant of it, leaving the communication worse than poor, for now it is wrong. Another reason that a poor interpreter may be worse than no interpreter is that the person who attempts to do the job may tarnish the reputation and trust that professional interpreters have worked so very hard to build. We are seen as a group, not only as individuals, and what each of us does influences the attitudes people have toward us as a whole.

If the interpreter has difficulty interpreting in certain situations, such as those involving a philosophical view very different than his or her own, then it is probably best to avoid such situations. Of course, if an interpreter were to find him- or herself in an uncomfortable situation, he or she would still be expected to do a professional job of transmitting the information presented. There is no excuse for the breach of ethics that altering the interpretation would represent. It is only human to be uncomfortable with situations that are foreign or in disagreement with our own sense of right and wrong; but it is the right of the consumers to determine their own sense of right and wrong, and to be exposed to whatever they choose in the manner it is presented. If the interpreter can maintain an impartial attitude, then he or she will be able to accept such interpreting assignments as these and possibly even enjoy them.

As a general rule, we have many associations with deaf people. Sometimes we are called upon to interpret in situations in which we are very familiar with some of the parties. If the interpreter is too close to the people involved, then it would be best to suggest that another interpreter serve. It is always nice to offer to help to find another interpreter and to explain the reason behind the refusal to interpret so as to maintain good relations. We may not do a thoroughly professional job interpreting for a parent, close friend, enemy or any other person who has too much of an impact on our lives, or when the situation is such that the outcome might affect the interpreter as well as the client. It is even difficult to do justice to the task when there are no personal repercussions, but one's feelings toward the individuals involved are strong.

If, for example, one were asked to interpret for his or her parent's divorce or that of a close friend, it would be extremely difficult to maintain any form of impartiality. Once an interpreter was interpreting for her grandfather's funeral and spent the entire time wishing that she were not the "cause" of her father's tears. Funerals create enough emotional stress for the interpreter without the added complication of being related to the parties involved. Sometimes it is helpful simply to know you have the right to turn down an interpreting assignment.

Compensation is a rather touchy topic and also requires discretion. It is up to the individual interpreter as to how to handle payment for services. Several institutions have already set up the machinery for compensation, and it would represent a step backwards to volunteer one's services in an area that has established a tradition of payment for interpreting services. Interpreters, deaf people, and professionals in deafness have invested a great deal of effort and time in the professionalization of interpreting. It would be a shame to block progress by accepting an unpaid position where the mechanism is already set up for payment. Educational interpreting, legal interpreting, and Vocational Rehabilitation interpreting are areas which usually offer pay.

There are several considerations in accepting volunteer status: could the interpreter be paid if someone would do some legwork and find a funding source; does the interpreter wish to volunteer; and is the interpreter able to remain professional regardless of the volunteer status of his or her interpreting? Often people resent feeling beholden to anyone and might really prefer to pay for the services of an interpreter or have the interpreting paid for by some other means. Volunteering is optional and should be handled as a choice rather than as an expected service. Interpreters should not allow themselves to feel pressured into interpreting when they may later resent it.

Professional Distance

Professional distance is the quality of caring about the clients one serves without allowing that to interfere with one's interpreting function, nor letting one's knowledge or information about clients affect one's outside life. We must be certain that the client who meets us at a social gathering does not spend the whole time wondering if we are acting differently because of our prior knowledge. Imagine the feelings of a deaf person at a deaf club meeting, for example, who meets the interpreter who was serving that afternoon in court for a hearing at which he was accused of infidelity to his spouse. It would certainly be an uncomfortable feeling in the first place, but would be even worse if the interpreter talked about the afternoon's experience, winked or gave some other indication that the two of them shared a naughty secret.

Similarly, our reaction to students' grades or response to a presentation or behavior of a client could be extremely inhibiting. If a student received a failing grade and the interpreter saw the grade, that might be embarrassing enough, but if the interpreter commented on it, that would surely worsen the embarrassment. By blushing at a client's behavior, we color the situation.

Another example of why professional distance is important is in the mental health setting. For instance, while waiting with a client for an appointment with a therapist, it is tempting to converse about the upcoming event. If such conversation were to occur, it is very possible that, having unloaded his or her feelings, the client might be less able or willing to do so again in the therapy situation. Some consumers, unsophisticated in the use of an interpreter, might be tempted to ask the interpreter to recap the conversation or to fill in gaps. Neither is tenable. Finally, this puts the interpreter in the difficult situation of holding information. This might tempt him or her to give advice, help or it simply might be difficult not to be able to react and interact within and after the counseling situation.

We are highly involved in any interpreting assignment. The important idea is to avoid allowing our involvement to become inappropriate.

Ethical Conduct

The first contact with consumers can set the stage for the entire association. Always be sure to introduce yourself to the parties involved when entering a new situation, so that everyone knows who you are and why you are there. The introduction should be concise and clear, stating your name and the function of an interpreter. It may also be wise to mention the referring party, such as the name of the interpreting coordinator of the Department of Vocational Rehabilitation. If the consumer is sophisticated in the use of an interpreter, he or she may prefer to do the introducing.

The four areas discussed help us to have a good overall idea of the code of ethics. In order for the code of ethics to have meaning, interpreters must understand and be able to explain or even defend its principles. Professionals cannot blindly follow a set of rules.

In order to maintain both the code of ethics and our public relations role, we must exercise tact. Often, out of ignorance, an individual will ask the interpreter for confidential information or to step out of his or her role. Even if the action is deliberate, the interpreter is probably much better off handling the whole affair as if it were not premeditated. When asked to step out of our professional role, the temptation is often to bark at the offender or to act self-righteously. It is probably best to gently but firmly explain the reason for refusal to agree to the request. When in doubt, educate. Another solution, of course, is to quickly change the subject or in some other way divert attention from the uncomfortable topic.

Central to the principles of ethical behavior is the necessity for interpreting faithfully the thought, intent and spirit of the people involved. The interpreter cannot alter the information or style for entertainment purposes, to help someone out, or because of personal opinion. The essential goal in interpreting is to make the situation equal, that is, an equal communication experience for the hearing and deaf people involved. By interpreting everything that is said and signed, all participants are fully involved in the communication and are appropriately made aware of the interpreter's function.

It is possible that the people involved might expect the interpreter to allow side comments or other information to pass. It is important to make it clear that the interpreter interprets everything, so that people do not act under erroneous assumptions. The interpreter might need to advise all parties in advance that everything will be interpreted. This is especially true in situations involving consumers who are unsophisticated users of interpreting services. Perhaps an introductory remark would be in order. The interpreter might say "My name is Mary Smith. I will be interpreting today. I will sign everything that is spoken and vocalize everything that is signed."

The interpreter is further called upon to avoid reacting to the content or style of the speaker or signer, so that the people relying on the interpreter for the information can form their own opinions. Some people react negatively to certain styles of presentation or to particular personalities. This can also be true for the information presented. Perhaps the real solution to not appearing judgmental is to try not to *be* judgmental while interpreting. Sometimes the concentration required helps not to show reactions by being too busy interpreting. To some degree it is possible to train oneself not to react. This training is evident in certain cultures in which a person must suffer a trial by pain without showing any reaction. In our own culture, people who are trained to be experimental observers develop the ability not to react so as not to affect an experiment while noting behavior.

There are many aspects of adherence to the code of ethics. Some general pointers to keep in mind are listed below. In discussing any aspect of interpreting, the interpreter must be certain to avoid naming people involved, places, dates, situations in detail, or any other particulars. It is possible that what may seem a very limited amount of information could be enough, if combined with another person's limited knowledge, to break confidentiality. Therefore, we must be cautious about sharing even what may seem to be unimportant or unenlightening facts. For example, if an interpreter were to say "Last month I interpreted for a divorce case, and the husband had to take three days off work. That's hard when you are a part-time worker, since they deduct from your paycheck." The previous sentences may seem relatively harmless, but there is danger in almost every word. Specifying the time, "last month," may be just the clue that lets someone know who was involved, along with the information that it was a divorce case. The facts that the husband had to take three days off work, that he has a part-time job and that money was deducted from his paycheck might be the information that would clearly tell someone exactly who was involved. A further complication is that it may be that the people involved would not wish people to know some of the details specified, such as the fact that the husband had to take three days off work, or that his job was part-time, or that they were getting a divorce.

Interpreters need to support one another. So often, people who do not understand the role or function of an interpreter will complain or gossip about the inadequacy of one interpreter to another interpreter. Sometimes this can be flattering to the person confided in; however, it is still important to maintain our faith in our colleagues. Often a misunderstanding causes such complaints, and we might be able to resolve the misunderstanding by clarifying the interpreter's role or by referring the complainer back to the interpreter involved.

Along this same vein, interpreters should try to discourage consumers confiding in them. We should not be the holders but the transmitters of information. If a consumer, for example, were to confide in the interpreter before an interpreting situation, that consumer might be tempted to ask the interpreter to then repeat the information to the other person involved in the interpreting situation.

We should not think of ourselves as experts on deafness, but rather refer the interested party to people who are experts. We are experts in communication and are able to answer many questions about the communication aspect of deafness, but we should avoid acting as experts in areas such as psychology as it relates to deafness or the education of deaf people. Posing as experts also relates to giving advice. This can be dangerous. If we give advice, we might be given the responsibility for ensuring action, so it is probably best to try to give as little advice as possible. So often we are seen as a good source of information because we are involved in many different aspects of deaf people's lives, including the interpretation of information from an expert, and may appear to know about the information being presented, since we function as the "hands" or "voice" of the expert. This leads to temptation on the part of the deaf or hearing client to turn to us for advice when really we are no better a source of information than any other lay person.

Summary

The Interpreter's Code of Ethics is the basic framework that has been established to protect interpreters and hearing and

deaf clients while using an interpreter. By thoroughly understanding this code, the interpreter is in a better position to make
the best decision in handling situations that come up in their
daily work. The code should also be the base for a philosophy
that an interpreter must develop in order to handle new and
different situations that arise. No two situations will be exactly
alike, and although role playing and discussion can help clarify
interpreter behavior, it is ultimately essential to develop a philosophy that forms the basis for decisions in various situations
that present themselves to us. We work with people and people
are never quite predictable.

Thought Questions

1. Explain why the Code of Ethics is important to our profession.
2. The underlying philosophy of the Code of Ethics is equal
   communication access. Give some examples of how the Code
   could ensure equality in communication for all persons involved.
3. What are the four major areas covered in the Code of Ethics?
4. Why are these four areas important to the rights of deaf
   people?
5. How does the Code of Ethics protect interpreters?
6. How would you handle a question from another interpreter
   about the outcome of a court case you had been interpreting?
   Why would you take the steps you outlined?
7. How might an interpreter avoid showing feelings of disapproval in an interpreting situation?
8. List some of the general points to keep in mind as an interpreter in thinking about the Code of Ethics.
9. How does the interpreter determine what information from
   a specific interpreting assignment can or cannot be shared?
10. What is the area in which an interpreter is expert?
11. List four considerations in accepting compensation or serv-
    ing as a volunteer.
12. On what occasions might an interpreter refuse to work on a
    volunteer basis?

13. What would you do if you were interpreting for a group therapy session and its members asked you to participate?
14. How would you handle a lecturer who used foul language?
15. List some situations that might be complex or difficult to handle. Using these situations, role play possible solutions.

Chapter 6

Sign-to-Voice Interpreting

Sign-to-voice interpreting is an extremely challenging task for the sign language interpreter. It is probably no harder than voice-to-sign interpreting, but hearing audiences, being generally less exposed to interpreters, rely differently on the interpreter than the average deaf audience. Because deaf clients are probably much more accustomed to receiving information through an interpreter, they are probably also able to watch interpreters with more ease and flexibility. Sign language interpreters are expected to put what they see into appropriate and precise English. This is another reason that the interpreter's command of both languages is important. Development of ASL and English vocabularies and grammatical principles cannot be over-emphasized.

Many interpreters feel that one of the ways they develop their sign-to-voice skills is through frequent association with the deaf community, because in this way they can practice the task of reading and understanding signs. Reading and actually transforming signed expressions into vocal expressions are, however, very different tasks. Receptive skill is essential to sign-to-voice interpreting, but the actual task of vocalizing must be practiced for effective interpretation. Sign-to-voice interpreting becomes even more important as more and more deaf people are actively contributing and responding rather than being only passive participants. We must work to make their expression as eloquent, or ordinary, in the vocal medium as it is in the visual.

Sign-to-voice interpreting is conveyed simultaneously, as is voice-to-sign or expressive interpreting. First person is always used, meaning that if the signer says "I want you to go over there," the interpreter will vocalize in the same person, "I want you to go over there."

Probably the best vantage point for the sign-to-voice interpreter is in the audience in front of the signer, with a microphone if necessary. Just as the voice-to-sign interpreter should not place him- or herself in front of a light source, so should the sign-to-voice interpreter make certain that the signer is not in front of a light source, that there is sufficient lighting, and that there are no distractions.

The sign-to-voice interpreter should remain as unobtrusive as possible. To some degree the interpreter is visually passive, rather than contributing extraneous visual information. Care should be taken not to overact visually or vocally. Rather, the voice should be modulated to the comfort level of the listeners and to the spirit of the signer.

It is important to speak loudly enough to be heard clearly even when your back is to the audience, yet not too loud for comfort. Interpreters should be careful not to mumble; rather they should pronounce loudly, clearly and carefully, unless the signer visually mumbles or whispers.

Sometimes interpreters copy signs of the signer while interpreting. This habit of mimicking can be very distracting. Within the signing population such behavior is often reserved for requests for repetition or clarification. For example, if the speaker signed "MY HOUSE THERE SMALL TOWN U-P-S-H-I-R-E," a reader could imitate the sign SMALL and the speaker might respond with "SMALL, 500 MAYBE 600 PEOPLE." If the reader imitated the sign TELEPATHY in an utterance like "MY FRIEND, ME TELEPATHY," the signer might spell M-E-N-T-A-L T-E-L-E-P-A-T-H-Y, or explain its meaning. Interpreters can use this knowledge in order to request repetition of a particular sign and as a precaution against using this technique inappropriately.

Some speakers have prepared speeches. If this is the case, ask for a copy and read it ahead of time; then synchronize the voicing with the signing. Timing is important: the impact should be as close to simultaneous as possible for the deaf and hearing participants. The eyes of the interpreter must be on the signer so that if the signer changes thoughts or interjects comments not on the paper, this can be interpreted. Some speakers might want or be willing to practice their speeches ahead of time and will allow the interpreter to practice with them. If there is the opportunity, it is wise to be as well prepared as possible; however, interpreting is a task of the moment and the interpreter must be prepared for any unplanned alterations in the presentation.

Choice of words and completeness are important skills for the sign-to-voice interpreter. The interpreter should let the signer lead sufficiently to be able to make sense of what is signed and to give the appropriate vocal expression and rhythm. If the signer emphasizes one sign, the vocal interpreter should give the same emphasis in his or her vocal interpretation. The interpreter should attempt to choose the most appropriate vocabulary for the signs presented.

There are many aids in the selection of appropriate English equivalents for signs. In making style choices, we should consider the age, sex and social class of the signer, and the setting can be of some assistance. One might imagine a middle-aged woman saying "delightful," but not "Mamma mia!" and a little boy saying "gosh" or "gee" or "wow," rather than "Oh, my dear Lord!" Cultural and environmental clues can be very helpful, yet the interpreter must in the end rely on his or her own sense of appropriateness in choice, because stereotypical responses only work in many, but not all, cases. There could be an occasional little old lady who might say "far out," or a bright child who could easily possess an erudite vocabulary beyond his or her years.

Lipreading is an essential skill for the sign-to-voice interpreter. It can help to make a much more precise interpretation and can often help the interpreter out of difficult situations when an unfamiliar sign appears. It can also assist in the reading of fingerspelling. Allow the facial and throat movements of the signer to assist in your interpreting and learn to trust and use your lipreading skills.

Grammar is also important. The sign-to-voice interpreter should use appropriate grammatical structures when vocalizing. One challenging grammatical structure is tense. Because ASL and English have very different ways of handling tense, this frequently results in errors in sign-to-voice interpreting. Maintain the appropriate tense throughout the utterance. For example, if the signer relates a story about his or her childhood and mentions that he or she wanted an ice cream cone, this should be spoken in the past tense, not "I want an ice cream cone." In ASL the past tense was established by the fact that the story is about the individual's childhood, i.e., "back when. . . . " Clearly the interpreter must be sophisticated in the grammar of both English and ASL in order to do a smooth interpreting job.

Nonverbal Cues

The sign-to-voice interpreter must be aware of the nonverbal elements of communication. Interpreters should be cautious not to show anxiety through body and facial expression. This is important for the client's confidence in the interpreter. It is also important so that the interpreter is not misread as disapproving of the signer's utterances. Facial and body expressions associated with discomfort can sometimes be misinterpreted as disapproval or anger. This could seriously affect the signer's comfort. In a similar manner, the facial expression that accompanies concentration, can be interpreted by the viewer as negative. For the sake of a comfortable atmosphere, we must be acutely aware of the nonverbal messages we send, even when sign-to-voice interpreting.

Vocal inflection and expression are also important in sign-to-voice interpreting. Interpreters should associate vocal cues with visual ones. Here again a large English and ASL vocabulary can be of help, so that the sign-to-voice interpreter selects the appropriate English equivalent for a sign. As mentioned earlier, vocalization should fit the signer's age, sex, social class, style, appearance, personality, and so forth. Beyond selection of vocabulary, slang usage and colloquial expressions, the interpreter will make nonverbal vocalizations based on the information about the signer. Sometimes a giggle will be a less appropriate vocalization than a guffaw or a chuckle. Certain expressions may call for a vocal "huh?" or "let me see," or a laugh or a gasp, for example.

Ethical Considerations

The ethics of sign-to-voice interpreting are the same as for the overall ethics of the field; however, some points should be emphasized here.

We must remember not to react either to the signer's information or to ourselves, such as when we make an error. If an error is made, it is probably best to correct it as quickly as possible and leave it at that. Too much apology can be intrusive and destroy the point of the speaker as well.

When the signer tells a joke, it may be appropriate for the interpreter to laugh, or giggle, but that laugh should be held until the end of the utterance, so that all the hearing participants will understand the joke before they hear any laughter.

Neither correct the signer nor add information to the spoken portion that is not expressed in the signed portion. We must transmit the words and spirit of the signer, which means being aware of vocal inflection and the body language and facial expression of the signer. In every interpreting situation we must transmit everything, even words and emotions which are not comfortable for us, such as swear words and anger, and topics that we sometimes feel strongly about.

Never criticize the signer as an excuse for a poorly executed interpreting job. This is sometimes tempting, but merely seems like "sour grapes" and puts the deaf person in a poor light. If the interpreting job was difficult, regard it as a challenge and maintain a professional exterior.

Sign-to-voice interpreting allows deaf people and hearing people the opportunity to interact more fully. We must develop skills and confidence, as well as comfort, in order to fill the need. As our skills grow, so will the quality of interchange and the comfort of those we serve.

Thought Questions

1. How can a sign-to-voice interpreter remain unobtrusive? List four ways.
2. What are four ways to determine the English word that should be spoken?
3. What is the benefit of allowing the signer some lead time in sign-to-voice interpreting?
4. List five physical considerations in sign-to-voice interpreting.
5. List and discuss six ethical considerations of sign-to-voice interpreting.
6. How can the sign-to-voice interpreter best transmit the facial expression, body language and other nonverbal aspects of the signing in his or her vocalization of the signer?

Chapter 7

Interpreting in Various Settings

All interpreting situations involve the code of ethics and the basic principles of the field. In this chapter we will look at some of the special considerations of common situations in which interpreters find themselves. These settings are as varied as the people we serve; yet we will try to discuss some of the more general points, keeping in mind that they may vary with each client.

Religious Settings

Interpreting in the religious setting may involve any number of experiences, from a simple religious service to a baptism, counseling session, wedding, funeral, bar mitzvah, or any number of other events. Generally, interpreting in the religious setting involves an audience rather than one-to-one interpreting. It is important to assess the audience for sign system preference. One likely choice might be ASL or Ameslish, since one cannot predict the makeup of a congregation or because the people might represent a mixture of systems. Be sure to check for signs used in the particular setting, as certain signs vary according to sect or religion. For example, "baptize" is signed differently by Catholics and Baptists, and Jews have a different sign for "bible" than Christians. If you check ahead, you can save yourself confusion or embarrassment. Good resources would be an experienced interpreter or a deaf member of that faith.

One commonly finds music in the religious setting. Interpreters must be prepared to interpret hymns and the like. If possible, read the appropriate section from a hymnal or songbook ahead of time and/or practice with the singer or choir, whether the program is live or taped. Work to express meaning and rhythm. Some interpreters leave the hymnal or music open in front of them in case they need to refer to it for words that are difficult to hear and to be ready for upcoming lines. When using such aids, try to continue giving the audience some eye contact.

RELIGIOUS INTERPRETING: TWO DIFFERENT POSITIONS

If a second language such as Hebrew, Arabic, or Latin is used, the interpreter is not generally expected to translate. Typically the interpreter signs "Hebrew word (or language)" or "Latin word. . . . " If the rabbi, minister, or priest has prepared an English translation for the interpreter, then the interpreter can follow the translation to sign to the audience while the other language is being spoken. Again, try to maintain some level of eye contact with the audience while reading.

Some or all of the sermon or service might be prepared ahead of time, in which case an interpreter may have the luxury of looking over the service before the event. This can be especially helpful for reading through any passages to be used from the *Bible, Torah, Koran,* or the like. Such passages may involve complex or poetic language, and preparation can assist in clearer interpreting.

The religious setting is a forum for many strong feelings. Since interpreters must always be true to the spirit of the speaker, it is for emphasis that we mention the following again. It is essential for the interpreter to transmit feelings accurately in his or her interpretation. It might be wise to avoid interpreting in a situation where the emotions of the interpreter might be too strong to allow the spirit of the speaker to flow through the interpreter.

Television and Artistic Performances

More and more segments of life are becoming accessible to deaf audiences, including such things as television and theatrical events. Songs and plays are performed in sign language, plays and motion pictures are interpreted. Even television news, interviews, and other programs sometimes include an interpreter.

Live artistic interpreting requires generally larger signs for visibility, and often signs are chosen for their aesthetic value, as well as for their meaning. Often interpreters in artistic settings need to practice ahead of time and interpret simultaneously with the spoken or sung words.

A greater amount of latitude is given an artistic interpreter to provide opportunities for creativity. The interpreter first decides

INTERPRETING FOR LIVE PERFORMANCE

upon an interpretation of the meaning of the piece and then upon how to sign that meaning. Individual situations will dictate how much or little freedom the interpreter has in determining his or her interpretation.

In certain art forms, such as poetry and music, rhythm will also play an important role. Interpreters may alter their interpretations slightly to accommodate the rhythm. Meaning is still most important and accommodations for rhythm, beauty, or impact should not alter or obliterate the meaning.

Television interpreting is a rapidly growing field for sign language interpreters. Many programs have interpreters, whether in inserts or as part of the onstage performance. If the interpreter is in an insert, one important precaution is keeping the interpreter's hands within the insert. Camera technicians are not always aware of the significance of an interpreter's hands and may cut out an important aspect of a sign. It might be wise to have a signer-adviser to watch and be sure the technicians don't cut out anything significant.

TELEVISION INTERPRETING: THREE APPROACHES

Since we never seem terribly large on television, it is important to sign and fingerspell clearly and as largely as is possible for the space at hand. It is sometimes suggested that one "cramp" one's signs in order to allow the camera to move in closer. In this way the interpreter will appear larger.[1] It is helpful to work with the camera crew. Interpreters need to learn about camera work, and camera operators need to learn about the work of the interpreter in order for both to be more effective.

Medical and Mental Health Settings

Medical and mental health interpreting are very sensitive areas. Confidentiality, as always, is important, but may take on even further significance due to the personal nature of medical and mental health care.

Sometimes the sex of the interpreter may be an important factor, as the client may feel more comfortable with an interpreter of the same gender. Caution and tact are imperative: interpreters must never react to the client or situation. Occasionally the medical or mental health problem may be shocking, unattractive, or embarrassing. Although internally one might react, it is essential not to stare (i.e., at the anatomical area being examined) or react visibly. If swearing or shocking language occurs, the interpreter must be prepared to transmit without reacting.

Pantomime or graphic gesturing may be useful techniques, but here again interpreters must exercise caution. Pointing at parts of the client's body should be avoided. It may be better to rely on pictures, picture books or three-dimensional models so as not to embarrass or degrade the client. Interpreters should avoid touching clients while interpreting.

Because information can be technical, unless the interpreter is trained in medical terminology, vocabulary should be handled cautiously. First, the interpreter should listen carefully, and any technical or unfamiliar words should be fingerspelled. The interpreter must not guess at meanings or even how to spell a word. It may be necessary to ask for repetition or for the spelling. Interpretation should be literal. For example, "you have the flu" should not be signed "YOU SICK" but rather "YOU HAVE F-L-U." In the case where the client does not understand, he or she has the responsibility of asking for clarification.

Deaf people should not have more responsibility than a hearing person might have. Hearing patients do not always ask questions directly, sometimes they look confused or sound confused. Interpreters can simulate this natural interchange by transmitting confused facial expressions and half-copied words or signs into the vocal mode by saying "Huh?" or "F-L-U?" without the consumer directly asking a question. It is not necessary to stop everything to formally ask a question. We often send messages through nods and questioning looks or remarks. It is important that the medical professional—not the interpreter—explain and answer any questions.

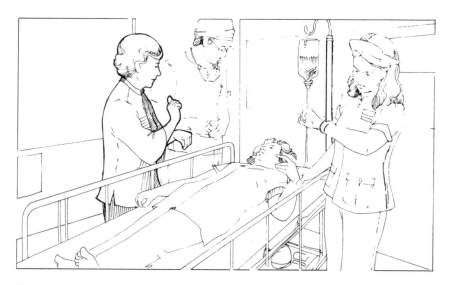

INTERPRETING IN THE MEDICAL SETTING

Several resources have listings of signs for medical situations. Woodward's *Signs of Sexual Behavior* and *Signs of Drug Use,* Babbini's *Manual Communication,* Madsen's *Conversational Sign Language II,* and the Department of Health, Education and Welfare publication, *Interpreting for Deaf People,* are five sources containing sections that pertain to terms that may come up in medical/mental health interpreting.

Mental health interpreting requires particular sensitivity to the fact that the interpreter may be an unwanted but necessary participant. Thus, using caution and tact is again essential. Interpreters must be careful not to appear to side with either therapist or client, and must also be cautious not to appear to assume the therapist's role. It might be necessary or helpful to explain the interpreter's role before beginning. At this time the client and therapist can be assured that the interpreter will transmit everything they say and that the interpreter will maintain confidentiality.

Sometimes consumers may use confusing language which may indicate their mental state. In these cases an interpreter needs to explain this to the therapist and interpret as accurately as possible without altering the client's language. It is essential here that the interpreter know the difference between ASL or some form of regular, common signing and poor or confused signing.

**INTERPRETING FOR A DOCTOR-PATIENT CONFERENCE
(MEDICAL OR MENTAL HEALTH SETTING)**

Sign-to-voice skill is a necessary component so that communication is not stifled. If conversation prior to a situation is needed to orient the interpreter and consumer to one another's signing, it is important to avoid discussing mutual friends or acquaintances. Although it is natural to discuss the upcoming event, avoid such discussion. However, if the client is persistent, explain why you can't talk about the case. There are many reasons why the interpreter cannot carry on a conversation regarding an upcoming event. It involves the interpreter personally and directly, and is outside of his or her function. If ever the interpreter becomes involved in even a simple conversation before or after an interpreting situation, or during a break, he or she should never sign without talking and never talk without signing. Trust is a very delicate quality, and is easily broken. It is very important that no one view the interpreter as taking sides or becoming involved in any way.

In medical or mental health situations it is possible that the interpreter might be tempted or even asked to handle questions related to deafness; however, this can lead to confusion of roles and can be dangerous. The interpreter can try to have a list of resources handy so that clients can contact experts on deafness.

Platform Interpreting

Interpreters often serve at large meetings, lectures, banquets and other events where a speaker and audience are involved. Generally, the phrase "platform interpreting" is applied to any situation where the speaker stands in front of an audience in a relatively formal manner. If the speaker is communicating vocally, the interpreter generally stands nearby. On rare occasions the interpreter may sit in the audience facing the deaf portion of the audience. In these situations the interpreter should be seen without effort. If the speaker is signing without voice, the interpreter is positioned in front and facing the signer, with a microphone if possible.

PLATFORM INTERPRETING

Usually the audience is farther away from the interpreter than usual, so physical factors are important. Signs are produced larger and fingerspelling is kept to a minimum. If a word must be fingerspelled, it should be done slowly and clearly. Hands must be kept slightly lower than usual if the interpreter is higher than the audience on a platform. This will allow lipreading and facial expression to be seen.

Lighting is also important. Interpreters should stand in the best light possible. If there is any choice, of course stand in a well-lit spot. Posture can help visibility. Again, because the audience is lower, the interpreter's chin should not be set too high. Good posture can provide a better background for signs and a better basis to help one sign larger. Eye contact, as always, is important for maintaining rapport with the consumers and is helpful for assessing one's effectiveness. If the interpreter notices discomfort or confused looks, an adjustment in choice of style and/or signs may be necessary.

Larger signing can be fatiguing and, therefore, platform interpreters only work for periods ranging from fifteen to thirty minutes at a stretch, trading with other interpreters. If possible, trading should be done when speakers change, for this is far less distracting. When interpreters are working together taking turns, the one who is resting should watch for signs of fatigue in the one who is working and spell the fatigued interpreter when necessary.

If it is necessary to trade interpreters while a speaker is talking, the fresh interpreter moves behind the working interpreter, tapping the working interpreter lightly to indicate readiness to take over. Then the fresh interpreter watches the working interpreter and listens to the speaker. When the working interpreter is ready, usually at a sentence break or pause, he or she will move out of the way and the new interpreter will pick up where the first interpreter left off. This routine should be practiced until it is smooth, before it is done in front of an audience.

It is helpful to be familiar with the format of a program so that interpreting can be planned efficiently. If there are many speakers, it is helpful to know how many and approximately how long each will speak. In some cases an interpreter can stay on the platform through several speeches, knowing the speeches will be short. Sometimes speakers sign for themselves. It can be embarrassing for an interpreter to stand up to interpret and then turn and sit back down because the speaker signs as well as speaks. It is also embarrassing to see a deaf speaker stand in front of an audience with no voice interpretation because no one can find the microphone. These factors should be attended to before the actual event.

Interpreters can prepare for platform interpreting by checking to see if speakers will use written speeches or outlines. If so, the interpreters can get a copy (or read over the speaker's copy if necessary) and study it ahead of time. Platform interpreters should not try to read while voice-to-sign interpreting, but may find it useful to read a signer's speech while sign-to-voice interpreting. In the latter case, the interpreter should read over the speech ahead of time and then follow it with an eye constantly on the signer to permit him or her to transmit facial expression, side comments, digressions, and other details not in the written speech. The interpreter should watch the signer also to be sure the voiced and signed speeches are simultaneous. It can destroy the effect of a speech to have the interpreter finish ten sentences before or after the signer.

Platform interpreting requires more preparation and effort for visibility. Larger signing, solid backgrounds (as always), and good lighting can all contribute to more effective service.

Educational Settings

With new laws and new policies, more and more educational experiences are being integrated. Deaf and hearing students are taking classes from hearing and deaf teachers. This has caused an explosive need for educational interpreters. Because of this need, many interpreters have full-time interpreting jobs. Interpreters are present in many educational settings: elementary and high schools, junior colleges, adult education programs, four-year colleges and universities, masters and doctoral programs, vocational and technical programs, and less formal educational programs.

Generally, the interpreter sits facing the deaf student at the front, to the side of the teacher and slightly in front of him or her. If possible, the interpreter should be positioned so that the deaf students can look past her or him to see the teacher without straining. This also applies to the use of visual aids. The interpreter should be positioned so as not to block visibility of visual aids and so that students can see both easily; sometimes this necessitates standing and even moving. Since movement is so dominant in signing, interpreters should try to use space and directionality as it relates to the visual aid. For example, if a map of the United States is being displayed and the teacher talks about pioneers traveling westward, the interpreter should sign "TRAVEL" in the direction that is west on the map. If they traveled north, the interpreter would sign "TRAVEL" with upward directionality, which again would allow the students' eyes

EDUCATIONAL INTERPRETING: SECONDARY OR POST-SECONDARY

EDUCATIONAL INTERPRETING: ELEMENTARY OR PRE-SCHOOL

to move to the right location and in the right direction. In the same sense, usually when the teacher talks about the right side, it is on the interpreter's left and vice versa. The interpreter should lead the eyes of the students correctly for the visual aid behind the interpreter, as if looking in a mirror. If the visual aid is a movie or slides, a small flashlight can be held by the deaf student and used to light the interpreter's hands and face. Interpreters should carry such a flashlight with them.

Typically, the educational interpreter uses a form of English on the hands, but specifically uses whatever system is required by the educators in that setting. There may be a policy that requires use of SEE$_2$ in one school and Bornstein's *Sign English* in another, or several systems, depending on the students or classroom. Since educators have additional responsibility regarding language development, they also tend to determine which system or systems are used. The interpreter will use whatever is required in a school. In colleges, universities, junior colleges, and technical vocational programs, interpreters generally use PSE, leaning more toward straight English in some cases and more toward ASL in others. Again the institution's policy might dictate which way the interpreters lean. Often technical terminology comes into play and for this reason technical signs are used. Sometimes there is no known technical sign. In these cases the clients and interpreter may agree upon an invented sign to use for that term or may fingerspell it. Interpreters must remember that these may well be temporary signs, not useful or understandable with any other client.

Sign language interpreters are essential to the application of the mainstreaming concept. They allow access to public education and are a vehicle for hearing and deaf individuals to interact.

Vocational Settings

Vocational interpreting may be defined as any interpreting in an occupational setting. An interpreter may be used when a deaf person is being hired or is hiring someone for a job, or when job preparation or on-the-job training is taking place. Because the Department of Vocational Rehabilitation is involved with clients getting jobs, interpreters often serve that department in job counseling, testing or training situations.

Dress can be important in vocational interpreting. Scarves or loose skirts can be dangerous around certain machinery and clothes could get dirty in some cases. In an office setting, the jeans that were perfect around machinery are inappropriate. Some people assume that the interpreter is a representative of deaf people. Ill-attired interpreters can harm such a person's attitude toward deaf people and/or use of interpreters in the future.

Technical terms may crop up that are familiar to people in a particular field but are new to the interpreter. Sometimes the interpreter can prepare by looking over books on a particular occupation. The signer may have a technical sign vocabulary that is greater than the interpreter, so the interpreter can pick up vocabulary from the client. While things are being demonstrated, it is a good idea to try to facilitate visibility by being as close as possible to the demonstration.

INTERPRETING FOR JOB INTERVIEW

INTERPRETING FOR VOCATIONAL TRAINING

Interpreting in vocational settings permits easy and comfortable communication between workers and management and among workers or among management, again allowing greater possibilities for integration. Some companies hire interpreters to work in their facilities full-time because they have so many deaf people in the firm.

Legal Settings

Any time the law is a factor, a situation could be called legal interpreting. This means interpreting where police are involved, in a courtroom, for attorney-client interviews, in jail or prison, with a probation or parole officer and so forth. Interpreters serve in both civil and criminal affairs. The National Registry of Interpreters for the Deaf has certification for legal interpreting, the Specialist Certification Legal (SC:L) (see Chapter 9, "Certification"). Legal interpreting requires knowledge of various legal settings, as well as skills in transmission of information. It is not an area to be taken lightly.

Legal interpreters are sometimes called upon to explain their role for the court. If this is the case, be brief and respectful. Any time anyone is addressed in court, they must respond. This may merely mean stating that the interpreter is unable to answer a question.

COURTROOM INTERPRETING

INTERPRETING BETWEEN LAWYER AND CLIENT

Being audible takes on new meaning in court. One must be audible enough for the court reporter to hear and take down the words. The interpreter should consider this in positioning. If the interpreter's back is to the recorder, it is possible his or her voice will be muffled and difficult to hear.

Orientation to the signer's system of communication is essential, as always. It may be a good idea to converse with the client to become oriented to his or her signing and to allow the client to become comfortable with the interpreter's signing. It is still essential to avoid discussion of anything related to the case at hand, for confidentiality only applies when we are interpreting. If no third person is present, the interpreter can be asked to give evidence on information obtained during such a conversation. Tremendous caution is recommended in any case where the interpreter is alone with a client. Both to avoid conversation and simply for a rest, the interpreter may find it easiest to isolate him- or herself during breaks. However, be certain to stay close by in case you are needed.

Sign language is highly visible. The interpreter can position him or herself in such a way that his or her signs are not visible to people other than the clients. Often lawyers and clients have quiet conversations in the hall outside the courtroom. It would be unfair if the interpreter signed so visibly that other signers could "eavesdrop" on the private conversation. In these cases the interpreter must exercise caution, signing in a whisper just as the lawyer speaks in low tones.

Terminology is an important factor in the legal setting. It is the lawyer's job to explain terms and legal consequences, but the interpreter must be prepared to clearly sign such explanations; therefore, familiarity with the terms and with the law will be of tremendous benefit to the interpreter. Likewise, the vocalization of information must be carefully handled. The interpreter works extra hard at accuracy and never assumes anything. It may be that responses are not necessarily coded in "signs" but may, in fact, be facial or gestural. If the deaf person nods, that is not vocalized as a "yes." The signer must use a sign that means YES. If a person gestures or points, the court interprets that vocally. For example, the judge may say, "the defendant is pointing to his right shoulder." The area of legal interpreting is complex and important. Interpreters should be well prepared and competent before accepting assignments in a legal setting.

Thought Questions

1. Which settings might generally require larger signing and minimal fingerspelling?
2. Which settings are generally one-to-one?
3. How can an interpreter prepare ahead of time for each of the settings described in this chapter?
4. How can interpreters handle music if it occurs in a religious or artistic setting?
5. How should an interpreter determine which sign system to use in each of the settings outlined in this chapter?

---

[1]Personal Communication, Barbara Reade (1980).

Chapter 8

Situations Calling for Special Skills

The stereotyped mental image of interpreting is an interpreter near a hearing speaker, facing one or more deaf persons. Other details may vary, but this is the general format. This chapter will deal with situations that don't quite fit this picture. We will be looking at telephone interpreting and interpreting where deaf-blind consumers, oral consumers or consumers with minimal language competence are involved. All of these cases require modifications of the ordinary interpreting format.

Telephone Interpreting

Since telephone interpreting is generally done on a one-to-one basis, the first thing to keep in mind is that the deaf client controls half of the event. The interpreter can ask the deaf consumer how he or she wishes to handle the situation. If the deaf person is placing the call, he or she can put the dime in the telephone, dial the number, and, in effect, do everything necessary other than hearing on the telephone. Perhaps the deaf person prefers to introduce the interpreter him- or herself.

The interpreter should get in the habit of signing everything, as a telephone conversation provides no visual information for the deaf individual. Interpreters transmit the fact that the telephone is ringing, each time it rings, a busy signal, laughter, pauses, etc. In the same sense, the interpreter is responsible for conveying all the visual information, such as smiles, reactions, or other nonverbal visual information received from the deaf client.

Many deaf persons are quite sophisticated in the use of a telephone and a telephone interpreter. Some, however, are not fully

TELEPHONE INTERPRETING: DEAF PERSON NOT USING OWN VOICE

aware of how to use an interpreter on the telephone; therefore, it might be helpful to clarify the options available. Some deaf clients use their own voices and may use the interpreter only as their ears while they speak for themselves. In such cases, earphones or a nearby telephone extension may be used. Other times the interpreter signs what is said and vocalizes signs, using first person so that the two clients talk to one another directly.

TELEPHONE INTERPRETING: DEAF PERSON USING OWN VOICE

At the close of a telephone conversation, the interpreter should not hang up without being directed to do so by the deaf party, and allowing time for the hearing and deaf clients to make any last remarks. Ideally the deaf person should tell the interpreter when to hang up, but if there is no direction, the interpreter should ask if both parties are finished before hanging up.

Oral Transmission

Although oral transmission is not sign language interpreting, it may be helpful to add a note about this sort of task, as it may be requested and because it may play a part in sign language interpreting. The oral task is the transmission of auditory input into the visual mode of lipreading accompanied by facial expression and body language. For optimum visibility, the face and neck should be clear of distractions, the hands should not cover any part of the face or neck, and the interpreter should be sure not to lean on his or her hands. In addition, the lighting should be good, especially on the face and neck. Scarves, lacey necklines, beards and moustaches can seriously reduce the visibility of the throat, lips and face for the lipreader. Another thing to be sensitive to is the color of the lips: they should be dark but not too bright.

ORAL TRANSMISSION

Oral transmission requires close proximity for clear visibility. Typically the oral facilitator sits in front of the deaf consumers to be served and silently transmits, on his or her lips, what is spoken. The reason oral transmitters are employed is because the speakers are often too far away for the oral deaf audience to lipread clearly. There are further skills an oral transmitter develops for specialization in this area, such as synonym usage for words that are easier to lipread.[1]

Tactile Interpreting[2]

Many methods are used to communicate with deaf-blind individuals. Tadoma is the technique of oral communication with a deaf-blind person through the use of the thumb on the lips for tactile lipreading and a finger on the throat to feel the vibrations of the vocal cords. Palm writing is a method in which one person draws out capital letters on the palm of the deaf-blind person to make words. A third method employs a special glove that has the letters of the alphabet in specific places on the palm. One person taps out words by pointing to the location of each letter on the glove. Some deaf-blind persons communicate by fingerspelling in one another's palms, while others sign and fingerspell in each other's palms. One other technique is to tap out the Morse code into the palm of a deaf-blind person, and another is to type to one another on a braille typewriter that has six balls which raise and lower to create braille that can be read at the moment it is being typed.

Some deaf people who are losing their vision or whose vision is not entirely impaired will grasp the other signer's wrists to follow the signing for assistance in focusing.

When using interpreters, deaf-blind individuals generally rely on tactile fingerspelling, tactile fingerspelling and signing, tactile typing, or the tracking described above, and sometimes prefer a combination of these techniques to avoid fatigue.

Deaf-blind interpreting is necessarily almost always done on a one-to-one basis, and the interpreter must transmit not only what is audible but what is visible as well. This presents a great challenge and requires a good deal of judgment, as well as skill, sensitivity and awareness.

Interpreting in a situation involving deaf-blind individuals can be very fatiguing, both mentally and physically. There is an

TACTILE INTERPRETING

added weight on the hands of the interpreter, and the position of the signer cannot change as often or as easily as when there is no one resting their hands on the interpreter's. The interpreter must be ingenious in finding ways to transmit visual and auditory input so that it is clearly readable and understandable. The interpreter must use his or her imagination to determine how things will feel in the palm of the deaf-blind person and how to express things from one mode, the visual or auditory, into another, the tactile mode.

In interpreting situations involving deaf persons, an interpreter can usually adjust information, technique and style as a response to the visual input from the deaf consumers in the audience, however there is often little or no feedback from a deaf-blind person while interpreting for that individual. Some deaf-blind individuals are not aware of the visual effect they have on others and do not emit ordinary visual signals; therefore, the interpreter must be prepared to determine the style, technique, and general approach based on other criteria, such as knowledge of the situation or client.

The tactile interpreter must try to transmit the visual information as well as auditory input. The interpreter must first identify him- or herself, then tell the deaf-blind person who else is in the room. It is also important to identify who is talking each time the speaker changes. Facial expression and other visual or auditory nonverbal information should also be interpreted.

Perhaps the deaf-blind client prefers the interpreter to express the nonverbal input, for example signing "SHE'S LAUGHING," or the deaf-blind person and the interpreter might devise a set of cues that indicate responses or facial, body and vocal expression. Manner of signing can also indicate some of the nonverbal portions of the utterance; e.g., sharp signing might show a speaker's crisp speaking style.

Timing is sometimes difficult in tactile interpreting, because it is seldom easy to interrupt and/or comment along the way. For example, often during an ordinary spoken conversation the listener will vocalize here and there, as a form of encouragement, things like "uh-huh," "really?" and other words, sounds or phrases. A signer in an ordinary signed conversation might sign "YES" or nod vigorously. This information is not easily accessible to a deaf-blind individual; so it might be wise for the deaf-blind person and the interpreter to work out a set of prearranged signals that can be used to respond to the speaker or to convey responses from listeners without interrupting.

Interpreting in a situation involving deaf-blind individuals is very challenging and requires a degree of sensitivity and judgment that is even greater than that required in general sign language interpreting.

Interpreting for Deaf People with Minimal Language Competency

There are some people who, because of inadequate education, lack of exposure to language, or many other reasons, are not competent in any language. This means that they use neither English nor ASL fluently. These people have been labeled low verbal or mentally retarded, or are said to have minimal language skills. It is probably best to use the least judgmental terms possible, such as minimal language competency. There is no necessary correlation between intelligence and the communication skills of these people. Some highly intelligent people have never been given a chance to demonstrate their intelligence through language. There are, however, others who do not have the mental capacity necessary for the sophisticated use of language. One cannot always tell level of intelligence upon meeting a person with minimal language competency and therefore should not judge.

While interpreting in situations with deaf individuals having minimal language competency, there are many things that might allow the interpreter to communicate more effectively with the individual. It is important to clearly identify who is talking and to whom. It is also important to establish the role of the interpreter, because many people may have never used an interpreter in the past. Some may have never even seen or heard of one.

It may be helpful to know that an interpreter can use any and all props in the room and rely on pointing whenever possible, as this is one of the clearest ways to refer to an object or person. Pictures can be very helpful. In fact some interpreters carry a picture book that shows a variety of concepts for quick and easy reference while interpreting. Often we can use rudimentary signs, such as "home signs", as well as ordinary gestures that are used and understood by signers and nonsigners alike. Finally, pantomime should be heavily incorporated into the interpretation for a graphic demonstration of the concept.

Where minimal language competency is involved, the interpreter should remember to constantly check for understanding at each completed thought before moving on. This also means checking the vocabulary used to be sure it is understood. A good policy is to rely on the vocabulary used by the deaf client. Often areas that are familiar to the deaf client may differ from those that are familiar to the interpeter.

Fingerspelling should be avoided because English may not be known by the deaf client involved; however, any fingerspelled words introduced by the deaf client certainly should be used. Without knowing English it is possible the client will know *some* English words, especially words he or she has seen often, such as STOP. However, the client may not understand script or even fingerspelling, so a printed word may occasionally help. The deaf client's facial expression can be watched as an indication of what is comfortable or understandable for him or her.

There is some temptation to treat deaf adults with minimal language competency like children because their language may seem childlike. We must treat them as adults and always give them the respect every adult deserves.

In reading information from a person with minimal language competency it is useful to keep in mind that not all nods of the head represent a "yes." Sometimes such a nod means, "yes, I understand"; other times a nod means "I'm being polite" or "I am listening/paying attention." Thus, it is important that the interpreter not vocalize a "yes" for a nod.

It is often helpful to first establish a baseline fact and ask questions based on that fact, such as "You live here now"; then "Where did you live last year?"

Time reference and time order should be carefully handled. We need to maintain consistency in tense and keep thoughts in time sequence as much as possible. It is usually helpful to keep tense as simple as possible and that means not switching tense, keeping time ordered events in their proper sequence, and clearly indicating any change in tense.

Facial and body expression of the interpreter are very important factors in minimal language competency interpreting. We must be concerned with how we affect the "interpreting climate" and try to create a comfortable environment for communication. While we must not try to change the atmosphere of the event, we should be sure we are not adding tension to it. Our faces and body language will be important in this respect.

Also facial expression and body language will be important in conveying the vocal expression of the speaker and in establishing the atmosphere intended by the speaker. We may find it difficult to display the proper expression if we show that we are working hard or are confused or frustrated. Once again it is important to control the nonverbal information sent.

Repetition and redundancy can be very helpful. Use repetition for clarity and to reiterate points that have already been discussed. Repeat vocabulary and phrases in new contexts. Repetition can be essential in questions, negatives, emphasis and to underscore key ideas.

Certainly interpreting in the minimal language competency setting has unusual challenges, and interpreting behavior must be modified to fit the need. Interpreting is not always simultaneous; in fact, it is often consecutive. Although the interpreter neither adds nor deletes anything from either client's information, the form of the interpretation is generally lengthy and very differently structured.

Summary

Interpreting in special situations is a topic which could continue indefinitely. Outlined here have been some of the more common situations in which an interpreter might serve. Certainly the ethics of interpreting remain the same, but certain modifications are necessary in the actual format. It will be important to have a bit of background information and to work on the specific skills required for such situations.

Thought Questions

1. What equipment can be used when interpreting for a deaf person who prefers to speak for him- or herself on the telephone?
2. Why should a sign language interpreter know about oral transmission?
3. List the communication methods used for interpreting where deaf-blind individuals are involved. Briefly describe these methods.
4. Why do deaf-blind clients sometimes prefer a combination of methods? How can this be beneficial to the interpreter as well?
5. List some bits of visual information the interpreter might need to transmit tactilely to a deaf-blind client.
6. Define minimal language competency.
7. List ten techniques that can be employed while interpreting for a deaf person with minimal language competency.

---

[1]An interpreter who is interested in oral transmission can contact the Alexander Graham Bell Association, Oral Deaf Adults Society or Registry of Interpreters of the Deaf for more information.

[2]Personal Communication, Theresa B. Smith and Marty Taylor, 1979.

Chapter 9

Certification and the Registry of Interpreters for the Deaf

As the profession of sign language interpreting grew, interpreters realized the need for an organization that would represent them nationwide. As a result of this recognized need, a workshop was held in 1964, in Muncie, Indiana, at Ball State Teachers College, where the Registry of Interpreters for the Deaf (RID) had its official start.[1] At this meeting some of the first guidelines were discussed and the term "professional" was applied to sign language interpreters. Until this time most interpreters were people who happened to know sign language and were willing to interpret. Often this was voluntary, and there were no interpreters whose major professional identification was with the task of interpreting, per se. Typically they were teachers of the deaf, children of deaf parents, or religious workers who knew sign language and therefore were called upon to help when a communication need arose. There was no guarantee of excellence or skill. Although many were highly skilled, there were also many who either lacked sophisticated skills or were unaware of ethical behavior in an interpreting situation.

Let me stress that their main function was typically something other than communication. Often counselors, for example, were called upon to interpret for their clients as well as to counsel them. As the need for interpreters grew and the requirements became more highly standardized, interpreters became concerned with the development of an organization that would nurture the growth of this young profession.

The concerned interpreters and other professionals who formed the Registry of Interpreters for the Deaf set about the task of determining the professional interpreter's role and functions, as well as establishing the guidelines within which the sign language interpreter should operate. They possibly foresaw the advent of a professional interpreter whose primary function would be serving as a communication link, rather than that function being secondary to some other responsibility. Those pioneers have set the stage for our profession's growth.

Possibly the most significant step the RID has taken since its inception has been that of establishing evaluation procedures for certification of interpreters. Certification is an essential factor in any profession, as the general public cannot be responsible for knowing what constitutes skill in any area that takes a great deal of training and/or knowledge. For example, few patients are prepared to determine the medical competency of their doctors and nurses, nor can clients judge the skills necessary to an audiologist. Likewise our clients cannot always know if we are truly competent.

Until recently in some areas, and still the case in other areas, an interpreter was anyone who called him- or herself an interpreter. Recognizing this weakness, the National Registry of Interpreters for the Deaf decided to establish a certification process. Materials were developed and local representatives were certified for state evaluation teams. Most states now have their own evaluation teams and carry on evaluations for certification at least once a year.

It should be stressed that certification, though a high honor, is merely the stamp of approval of basic skills. It indicates the basic ability to serve in the capacity of a sign language interpreter. There is no guarantee that the interpreter who receives his or her certification can adequately serve in every situation he or she encounters, but certification implies that he or she can serve in almost any situation. Certification is like getting a driver's license. Just as the driver's license gives the driver the right to drive on our streets and certifies basic competency behind the wheel, so RID certification establishes the basic competency of the sign language interpreter to interpret in most situations. It does not distinguish between various levels of interpreters, just as a driver's license does not qualify anyone for the "Indy 500."

However, anyone who drives in the Indy 500 does first need to have a driver's license.

The purpose of the evaluation is to attempt a fair examination of both the skills and professionalism of the interpreter-candidate. An interpreter can presently be evaluated and certified in four general areas during one examination, two specialized areas of interpreting, and at the master's level. Certificates can be earned in the following areas:

1. Transliteration Certificate (TC): indicates skill in signing in English order when transmitting information.
2. Interpretation Certificate (IC): used to certify skill in the transmission of material by the use of ASL with minimal fingerspelling.
3. Reverse Skills Certificate (RSC): demonstrates the interpreter's ability to read ASL and signed English and transmit them into spoken English (Sign-to-voice).
4. Comprehensive Skills Certificate (CSC): indicates skill in all of the above areas and at a higher level of competence.

Once an interpreter has earned his or her CSC, there are specialized certificates which may be attempted in the following areas:[2,3]

1. Master Comprehensive Skills Certificate (MCSC): indicates competence at a higher and more experienced level in all aspects of the CSC; taken after at least four years of holding a CSC.
2. Specialist Certificate: Legal (SC:L): evaluates specific skills, vocabulary and knowledge as they relate to interpreting in the legal setting.
3. Special Certificate: Performing Arts (SC:PA): indicates competence in specific skills, vocabulary and knowledge as they relate to interpreting plays, poetry, music and the like.

Two provisional forms of certification are also available: the Provisional Permit (PP) and the Legal Provisional Permit (LPP). Both are effective for a maximum period of one year. Holders of these permits are expected to be evaluated for permanent certification by the end of that year. These certificates are given to working interpreters with intentions of becoming certified. The Provisional Permit should lead to Transliteration, Interpretation, Reverse Skills or Comprehensive Skills Certification while the LPP is for those interpreters working in the legal setting who will eventually undergo evaluation for the Specialist Certificate: Legal.

For both the Transliteration and Interpretation certification evaluations (TC & IC), the candidate must pass a minimum percentage of the sign-to-voice evaluation, although the standard is slightly lower than for the RSC or CSC. The thinking here is that the interpreter who interprets from voice to sign most of the time will still be called upon occasionally to interpret from sign to voice, such as when a deaf individual wishes to ask a question or make a brief statement.

There are five members on the evaluation team. These members must be approved by the National RID. Two of these five are hearing interpreters who hold Comprehensive Skills certificates and three are deaf members who hold Reverse Skills certificates. A sixth member of the team is a CSC interpreter who helps in the warm-up room and serves the evaluation board by signing exactly what the candidate is vocalizing in the sign-to-voice (reverse) portion of the examination so that the deaf members of the board can know how the candidate performed on that section.

INTERPRETER TAKING RID EVALUATION

The process of evaluation begins with a warm-up session for the candidate. The individual to be evaluated sits in a warm-up room to get accustomed to working with the kinds of materials that will be used during the evaluation. Warm-up can last from half an hour to a full hour.

After warm-up, the formal portion of the evaluation begins with an interview of the candidate by the board. The purpose of this section is for the board to rate appearance, attitude, professionalism, ethics and knowledge of the field. At the end of the interview the candidate will be asked to expressively translate, from an audiotape, spoken English into signed English. The next segment of the evaluation is to expressively interpret spoken English from an audiotape into ASL.

Following the expressive portion of the examination, the candidate will be evaluated on his or her sign-to-voice skill. Working from films or videotapes, the interpreter will vocally interpret from both ASL and signed English into appropriate spoken English. If a deaf person is being evaluated, then modifications are made so that the candidate can operate in some manner that is both practical and comfortable for that individual, whether using his or her voice, signed English, or written communication. This is determined with the help of the team chairperson.

All scores and opinions of the board are confidential and are not even discussed among the members themselves. Evaluation forms are then sent to the National RID office for computer analysis, at which time the final determination is made as to whether certification is awarded and at what level. The results are then sent to the candidate. No feedback is given to the candidate during the evaluation.

The NRID has attempted to create as objective an evaluation as possible. Board members work very hard at removing personal prejudices while evaluating, and they are able to step down if for any reason they feel they cannot be objective. The computer is also set up to eliminate scores that may indicate a biased point of view; that is, the score of any individual evaluator that varies greatly from the scores of the rest of the team will be eliminated automatically so that one person's scores cannot heavily influence the outcome of an evaluation. Similarly, if one evaluator's scores are consistently higher or lower than those of the other members of the team, his or her scores are also eliminated.

In order to be evaluated, one must pay an evaluation fee. The fee for evaluation varies according to level of certification attempted.

Evaluation is an important step in the professionalism of our field. It is hoped that all of us will make certification one of our goals and that we continue to strive to improve even after reaching that goal. Certification is a valuable tool for people both within and outside of our profession.

Thought Questions

1. Where were interpreters found before the Ball State Teachers College convention?
2. What major change has occurred since the introduction of the RID to the function of an interpreter?
3. Why do we need a Registry of Interpreters for the Deaf?
4. What are some of the values of certification of interpreters?
5. What does certification indicate in terms of skill?
6. What aspects of interpreting are examined in the certification process?
7. Name five certificates that exist at this time.
8. Write out three possible questions relating to the ethics of interpreting that could be asked in an evaluation for certification.
9. What other aspects of the interpreter are evaluated during the interview portion of the evaluation besides ethics?
10. Describe the process of evaluation for certification and outline particulars that the interpreter might keep in mind in each section.

---

[1]*Interpreting for Deaf People,* United States Department of Health, Education, and Welfare (Washington, D.C., 1965), p. 3.

[2]At the present time, the National Registry of Interpreters for the Deaf is developing other specialized certificates, including one in the area of Education Interpreting (1980).

[3]NRID, in cooperation with the Alexander Graham Bell Association, has also instituted certification for the Oral transmission task (1980). The certificates are: (a) Oral Interpretation Certificate: spoken to visible (OIC:S/V), (b) visible to spoken (OIC:V/S) and (c) Comprehensive (OIC:C). Terminology can be confusing here in terms of the definition of *interpreting.* Perhaps this will be clarified as the NRID looks more deeply into this topic.

Appendix A

Registry of Interpreters for the Deaf, Inc. Code of Ethics

The Registry of Interpreters for the Deaf, Inc. refers to individuals who may perform one or more of the following services:

Interpret

Spoken English to American Sign Language
American Sign Language to Spoken English

Transliterate

Spoken English to Manually Coded English/Pidgin Sign English
Manually Coded English/Pidgin Sign English to Spoken English
Spoken English to Paraphrased Non-audible Spoken English

Gesticulate/Mime, etc.

Spoken English to Gesture, Mime, etc.
Gesture, Mime, etc. to Spoken English

The Registry of Interpreters for the Deaf, Inc. has set forth the following principles of ethical behavior to protect and guide the interpreter/transliterator, the consumers (hearing and hearing-impaired) and the profession, as well as to insure for all, the right to communicate.

This Code of Ethics applies to all members of the Registry of Interpreters for the Deaf, Inc. and all certified non-members.

While these are general guidelines to govern the performance of the interpreter/transliterator generally, it is recognized that there are ever increasing numbers of highly specialized situations that demand specific explanation. It is envisioned that the R.I.D., Inc. will issue appropriate guidelines.

This Appendix included courtesy of NRID, Inc.

CODE OF ETHICS

INTERPRETER/TRANSLITERATOR SHALL KEEP ALL ASSIGNMENT-RELATED INFORMATION STRICTLY CONFIDENTIAL.

Guidelines:

Interpreter/transliterators shall not reveal information about any assignment, including the fact that the service is being performed. Even seemingly unimportant information could be damaging in the wrong hands. Therefore, to avoid this possibility, interpreter/transliterators must not say anything about any assignment. In cases where meetings or information becomes a matter of public record, the interpreter/transliterator shall use discretion in discussing such meetings or information.

If a problem arises between the interpreter/transliterator and either person involved in an assignment, the interpreter/transliterator should first discuss it with the person involved. If no solution can be reached, then both should agree on a third person who could advise them.

When training new trainees by the method of sharing actual experiences, the trainers shall not reveal any of the following information:

name, sex, age, etc. of the consumer

day of the week, time of the day, time of the year the situation took place

location, including city, state or agency

other people involved

unnecessary specifics about the situation

It only takes a minimum amount of information to identify the parties involved.

INTERPRETER/TRANSLITERATORS SHALL RENDER THE MESSAGE FAITHFULLY, ALWAYS CONVEYING THE CONTENT AND SPIRIT OF THE SPEAKER, USING LANGUAGE MOST READILY UNDERSTOOD BY THE PERSON(S) WHOM THEY SERVE.

Guidelines:

Interpreter/transliterators are not editors and must transmit everything that is said in exactly the same way it was intended. This is especially difficult when the interpreter disagrees with what is being said or feels uncomfortable when profanity is being used. Interpreter/transliterators must remember that they are not at all responsible for what is said, only for conveying it accurately. If the interpreter/transliterator's own feelings interfere with rendering the message accurately, he/she shall withdraw from the situation.

While working from Spoken English to Sign or Non-audible Spoken English, the interpreter/transliterator should communicate in the manner most easily understood or preferred by the deaf and hard of hearing person(s), be it American Sign Language, Manually Coded English, fingerspelling, paraphrasing in Non-audible Spoken English, gesturing, drawing, or writing, etc. It is important for the interpreter/transliterator and deaf or hard of hearing person(s) to spend some time adjusting to each other's way of communicating prior to the actual assignment. When working from Sign or Non-audible Spoken English, the interpreter/transliterator shall speak the language used by the hearing person in the spoken form, be it English, Spanish, French, etc.

INTERPRETER/TRANSLITERATORS SHALL NOT COUNSEL, ADVISE, OR INTERJECT PERSONAL OPINIONS.

Guidelines:

Just as interpreter/transliterators may not omit anything which is said, they may not add anything to the situation, even when they are asked to do so by other parties involved.

An interpreter/transliterator is only present in a given situation because two or more people have difficulty communicating, and thus the interpreter/transliterator's only function is to facilitate communication. He/she shall not become personally involved because in so doing he/she accepts some responsibility for the outcome, which does not rightly belong to the interpreter/transliterator.

INTERPRETER/TRANSLITERATORS SHALL ACCEPT
ASSIGNMENTS USING DISCRETION WITH REGARD TO
SKILL, SETTING, AND THE CONSUMERS INVOLVED.

Guidelines:

Interpreter/transliterators shall only accept assignments for
which they are qualified. However, when an interpreter/
transliterator shortage exists and the only available
interpreter/transliterator does not possess the necessary skill for
a particular assignment, this situation should be explained to
the consumer. If the consumers agree that services are needed
regardless of skill level, then the available interpreter/
transliterator will have to use his/her best judgement about accepting or rejecting the assignment.

Certain situations may prove uncomfortable for some
interpreters/transliterators and clients. Religious, political, ra-
cial or sexual differences, etc., can adversely affect the facilitat-
ing task. Therefore, an interpreter/transliterator shall not accept assignments which he/she knows will involve such situations.

Interpreter/transliterators shall generally refrain from providing services in situations where family members, or close personal or professional relationships may affect impartiality, since
it is difficult to mask inner feelings. Under these circumstances,
especially in legal settings, the ability to prove oneself unbiased
when challenged is lessened. In emergency situations, it is
realized that the interpreter/transliterator may have to provide
services for family members, friends, or close business associ-
ates. However, all parties should be informed that the
interpreter/transliterator may not become personally involved
in the proceedings.

INTERPRETER/TRANSLITERATORS SHALL REQUEST
COMPENSATION FOR SERVICES IN A PROFESSIONAL
AND JUDICIOUS MANNER.

Guidelines:

Interpreter/transliterators shall be knowledgeable about fees
which are appropriate to the profession, and be informed about
the current suggested fee schedule of the national organization.

A sliding scale of hourly and daily rates has been established for interpreter/transliterators in many areas. To determine the appropriate fee, interpreter/transliterators should know their own level of skill, level of certification, length of experience, nature of the assignment, and the local cost of living index.

There are circumstances when it is appropriate for interpreter/transliterators to provide services without charge. This should be done with discretion, taking care to preserve the self-respect of the consumers. Consumers should not feel that they are recipients of charity. When providing gratis services, care should be taken so that the livelihood of other interpreter/transliterators will be protected. A free-lance interpreter/transliterator may depend on this work for a living and therefore must charge for services rendered, while persons with other full-time work may perform the service as a favor without feeling a loss of income.

INTERPRETER/TRANSLITERATORS SHALL FUNCTION IN A MANNER APPROPRIATE TO THE SITUATION.

Guidelines:

Interpreter/transliterators shall conduct themsleves in such a manner that brings respect to themselves, the consumers and the national organization. The term "appropriate manner" refers to:
  (a) dressing in a manner that is appropriate for skin tone and is not distracting
  (b) conducting oneself in all phases of an assignment in a manner befitting a professional.

INTERPRETER/TRANSLITERATORS SHALL STRIVE TO FURTHER KNOWLEDGE AND SKILLS THROUGH PARTICIPATION IN WORKSHOPS, PROFESSIONAL MEETINGS, INTERACTION WITH PROFESSIONAL COLLEAGUES AND READING OF CURRENT LITERATURE IN THE FIELD.

INTERPRETER/TRANSLITERATORS, BY VIRTUE OF MEMBERSHIP IN OR CERTIFICATION BY THE R.I.D., INC., SHALL STRIVE TO MAINTAIN HIGH PROFESSIONAL STANDARDS IN COMPLIANCE WITH THE CODE OF ETHICS.

October, 1979

Resource Bibliography

Anthony, David. *Seeing Essential English*. Greeley: University of Northern Colorado, 1971.

Babbini, Barbara E. *An Introductory Course in Manual Communication; Course of Study Outline for Instructors*. Northridge, CA: National Leadership Training Program in the Area of the Deaf, San Fernando Valley State College (now California State University, Northridge), 1964.

Babbini, Barbara E. *Manual Communication: Fingerspelling and the Language of Signs*. Urbana, IL: University of Illinois Press, 1974.

Babbini, Barbara E. *The Effects of Fatigue on the Competence of Interpreters*. Northridge, CA: National Leadership Training Program in the Area of the Deaf, California State University, Northridge, 1969.

Baker, Charlotte and Padden, Carol. *American Sign Language: A Look at Its History, Structure, and Community*. Silver Spring, MD., T. J. Publishers, 1978.

Bearden, Carter E. *Handbook for Religious Interpreters for the Deaf*. Atlanta, GA: Home Mission Board of the Southern Baptist Convention, 1975.

Bearden, Carter, ed. *Manual for Religious Interpreters*. Atlanta, GA: Home Mission Board of the Southern Baptist Convention, 1975.

Bearden, Carter, ed. *Manual for Religious Interpreters*. Atlanta, GA: Home Mission Board of the Southern Baptist Convention, 1974.

Bird, Barbara J. and Smith, T. Michael. *Communication Needs of Deaf People in Industry*. (Technical Report #2). Rochester, NY: National Technical Institute for the Deaf, Interpreter Education Program.

Bjorlie, Henry O.; Galloway, Victor H.; and Beauchamp, Jane, eds. *Proceedings of a Conference for Teachers and Interpreters in Adult Education Programs for the Deaf.* Northridge, CA: National Leadership Training Program in the Area of the Deaf, San Fernando Valley State College (now California State University, Northridge), 1966.

Bornstein, Harry, *Sign English Dictionary for Preschool and Elementary Levels.* Washington, DC: Gallaudet College Press, 1975.

Brasel, Barbara B. and Brasel, Kenneth. "The R.I.D. Scoring System and How It works." *Journal of Rehabilitation of the Deaf* 7:3:76–79.

Brasel, Barbara B. and Brasel, Kenneth. "The R.I.D. Scoring System and How It works." *Journal of Rehabilitation of the Deaf* 7:3:76–79.

Brasel, Barbara B.; Montanelli, Dale S.; and Quigley, Stephen. "The Component Skills of Interpreting as Viewed by Interpreters." *Journal of Rehabilitation of the Deaf* 7:4:20–28.

Brasel, Ken and Shipman, John. *A Pilot Study to Explore Evaluation Techniques for Interpreters.* Northridge, CA: National Leadership Training Program in the Area of the Deaf, San Fernando Valley State College (now California State University, Northridge), 1969.

Burch, Daniel D. *A Status Report of Program Development and Activities of the Interpreter Training Program at the University of Arkansas at Little Rock.* Little Rock: University of Arkansas Interpreter Training Program, 1979.

Caccamise, Frank. "New Myths to Replace Old Myths?" in "Comments, Questions and Answers," A. B. Crammatte, ed. *American Annals of the Deaf* 123:513–515.

Caccamise, Frank et al. Signing, Speaking, and Interpreting (draft). Rochester, NY: National Technical Institute for the Deaf, 1979.

Caccamise, Frank and Blasdell, Richard. "Reception of Sentences Under Oral-Manual Interpreter and Simultaneous Test Conditions." *American Annals of the Deaf* 122:414–421.

Carter, S. Melvin and Lauritsen, Robert. "Interpreter Recruitment, Selection and Training." *Journal of Rehabilitation of the Deaf* 7:3:52–63.

Charlip, Remy and Miller, Mary Beth. *Handtalk; An ABC of Finger Spelling and Sign Language.* New York, NY: Parent's Magazine Press, 1974.

Chatoff, Michael. "Legal Interpreting." *Journal of Rehabilitation of the Deaf* 9:3:22–24.

Congrat-Butler, Stefan, compiler and ed. *Translation and Translators: Encyclopedia, Index, Register.* New York, NY: R. R. Bowker Co., 1979.

Cornett, R. Orin. *Cued Speech and "Total Communication."* Washington, DC: Model Secondary School for the Deaf, 1978.

Council of Directors (of the six federally stipulated postsecondary programs for the deaf). *Policies, Procedures and Guidelines for the Implementation of the National Interpreters for the Deaf Training Act of 1978.*

Council of State Administrators of Vocational Rehabilitation. *VR Agency Practices Regarding Payment for Interpreter Services in Postsecondary Education: Results of a Questionnaire Survey.* Washington, DC, 1979.

Crittenden, Jerry. "Psychology of Deafness: Some Implications for the Interpreter." *Journal of Rehabilitation of the Deaf* 8:4:19–23.

Danish National Association of the Deaf. *The Development of Interpretation as a Profession* (second international symposium on interpretation of sign languages, August 1977).

Davis, Hallowell and Silverman, S. Richard. *Hearing and Deafness.* Fourth Edition. New York, NY: Holt, Rinehart and Winston, 1978.

Daynes, Byron W. *The Court Interpreter.* Chicago, IL: The American Judicature Society, 1967.

Deninger, Michael; Cowan, Nancy; and Rosen, Roslyn. IIEP: Purpose, Contents, Participants, Processes: in *PL 94–142 and Deaf Children* (special issue of the *Gallaudet Alumni Newsletter*). Washington, DC: Gallaudet College, 1977.

Dicker, Leo. "Intensive Interpreter Training." *American Annals of the Deaf* 121:312–320 and 363.

DiPietro, Loraine. *Proceedings: The First Convention of the Registry of Interpreters for the Deaf* (Delavan, WI, 1970). Washington, DC: Registry of Interpreters for the Deaf, 1971.

DiPietro, Loraine. "Registry of Interpreters for the Deaf." *Hearing Speech News* 38:3:8–9.

Domingue, Rita and Ingram, Betty. "Sign Language Interpreta-
    tion: The State of the Art" in D. Gerver, and H. W. Sinaiko,
    eds. *Language Interpretation and Communication.* New York,
    NY: Plenum Press, 1978.
DuBow, Sy. "Federal Actions on Interpreters and Telecommuni-
    cations." *American Annals of the Deaf* 124:93–96.
East Bay Counseling and Referral Agency for the Deaf. *Report of
    Interpreters' Workshop I, Northern California,* 1968. Berkeley,
    CA.
Elmer, L. A. "What is a Good Interpreter?" *American Annals of
    the Deaf* 93:545.
Fant, Louie J. *Ameslan; An Introduction to American Sign Lan-
    guage.* Silver Spring, MD: National Association of the Deaf,
    1972.
Fant, Louie J. "The California State University-Northridge Ap-
    proach to Training Interpreters." *Journal of Rehabilitation of
    the Deaf* 7:3:44–47.
Fant, Louie J. "The CSUN Approach to the Training of Sign
    Language Interpreters." *The Deaf American* 25:3:56–57.
Fant, Louie J. *Intermediate Sign Language.* Northridge, CA:
    Joyce Media, Inc., 1980.
Fant, Louie J. *Say It With Hands.* Washington, DC: Gallaudet
    College, 1964.
Fant, Louie J. *Sign Language.* Northridge, CA: Joyce Media,
    Inc., 1977.
Federlin, Tom. "Sign Language Interpreters . . . The Changing
    Role." *The Deaf American* 31:3:17–18.
Flathouse, Virgil E. *Testing the Feasibility of Using Videotape in
    the Evaluation of Interpreters for the Deaf.* Northridge, CA:
    National Leadership Training Program in the Area of the
    Deaf, San Fernando Valley State College (now California
    State University, Northridge), 1967.
Fleischer, Lawrence. *Sign Language Interpretation Under Four
    Conditions* (unpublished doctoral dissertation, Brigham
    Young University). Salt Lake City, UT, 1975.
Flu, J. et al. *A Handbook for Interpreters.* Northridge, CA:
    California State University, Campus Services for the Deaf
    (now Support Services to Deaf Students).
Foret, Agnes and Petrowske, Mildred. *A Manual and Dictionary
    of Legal Terms for the Interpreters for the Deaf.* Detroit, MI:

Wayne State University Law School, Center for the Administration of Justice, 1976.

Garretson, Mervin, "Concept of the Least Restrictive Environment" in *PL 94–142* and Deaf Children (special issue of the *Gallaudet Alumni Newsletter)*. Washington, DC: Gallaudet College, 1977.

George, B. F. "Legal Status of Interpreting for the Deaf" in A. Foret and M. Petrowske, eds. *A Manual and Dictionary of Legal Terms for Interpreters for the Deaf.* Detroit, MI: Wayne State University Law School, Center for the Administration of Justice, 1976.

Gilbart, Helen. *Legal Seminar and Mock Trial.* Clearwater, FL: Florida Registry of Interpreters for the Deaf, 1972.

Godin, Lev. "Interpreters for the Deaf in Russia" (Grozny, translator). *American Annals of the Deaf* 112:95–97.

"Guidelines for the Preparation of Oral Interpreters: Support Specialists for Hearing-Impaired Individuals." *Volta Review* 81:135–145.

Guillory, LaVera M. *Expressive and Receptive Finger-Spelling for Hearing Adults.* Baton Rouge, LA: Claitor's Publishing Division, 1966.

Gustason, Gerilee; Pfetzing, Donna; and Zawolkow Esther. *Signing Exact English.* Silver Spring, MD: National Association of the Deaf, 1975.

Holcomb, Roy and Corbett, Edward, Jr. *Mainstream —The Delaware Approach.* Newark, DE: Newark School District, 1975.

Holcomb, Roy and Dreger, Dorothy. *Integration and Interchange of Deaf and Hearing Elementary Children.* Santa Ana, CA: Santa Ana Unified School District, 1972.

Hovland, Carroll. "Literature Can Live Through Signs." *American Annals of the Deaf* 120:558–564.

Hughes, Virginia; Wilkie, Faye; and Murphy, Harry. "The Use of Interpreters in the Integrated Liberal Arts Setting." *Journal of Rehabilitation of the Deaf* 7:3:17–20.

Hurwitz, T. Alan. *Principles of Interpreting.* Rochester, NY: National Technical Institute for the Deaf.

Ingram, Robert. "A Communication Model of the Interpreting Process." *Journal of Rehabilitation of the Deaf* 7:3:3–10.

Ingram, Robert. *Brain Mechanisms for Simultaneous Interpretation of Signed and Spoken Languages* (unpublished paper). Providence, RI: Brown University, 1978.

Ingram, Robert. "Letter to the Editor." *The Deaf American*
    30:5:25– 26.
Ingram, Robert. *Preliminaries to the Study of Bilingualism in
    Hearing Children of Deaf Parents* (unpublished paper). Provi-
    dence, RI: Brown University, 1976.
Ingram, Robert. *Providing Services to Deaf Clients: The Role of
    the Interpreter* (unpublished paper delivered at Third National
    Symposium, National Association of Social Workers, New Or-
    leans, 1972). Silver Spring, MD: Registry of Interpreters of the
    Deaf.
Ingram, Robert. "Scientific Theory in Interpretation and
    Rehabilitation— With Special Reference to the Severely
    Handicapped Deaf" in *Deafness Annual V*. Silver Spring, MD:
    American Deafness and Rehabilitation Association, forthcom-
    ing.
Ingram, Robert. "Sign Language Interpretation and General
    Theories of Language, Interpretation and Communication" in
    D. Gerver and H. W. Sinaiko, eds. *Language Interpretation
    and Communication*. New York, NY: Plenum Press, 1978.
Ingram, Robert. "Teaching Deaf Students How to Purchase and
    Use Interpretation Services." *The Deaf American* 29:9:3– 6.
Ingram, Robert. *The International Organizing Committee for the
    Third International Symposium on Interpretation of Sign
    Language* (unpublished paper presented at Eighth World
    Congress of the World Federation of the Deaf, Varna, Bul-
    garia, 1979).
Ingram, Robert. *The Proceedings: Conference on Preparation of
    Personnel in the Field of Interpreting*. Washington, DC: Gal-
    laudet College, 1972.
Ingram, Robert and Ingram, Betty, eds. *Hands Across the Sea:
    Proceedings of the First International Conference on Interpret-
    ing*. (Washington, DC: 1975). Washington, DC: Registry of
    Interpreters for the Deaf.
Interpreting for the Deaf in the Legal Setting: A Conference for
    Interpreters, Northridge, CA: San Fernando Valley State Col-
    lege (now California State University, Northridge), 1967.
Jacobs, L. Ronald. "The Efficiency of Interpreting Input for
    Processing Lecture Information by Deaf College Students."
    Journal of Rehabilitation of the Deaf 11:2:10– 15.
Johns, W. Lloyd. *Legal Interpreting for Deaf Persons, A Course
    Outline*. Northridge, CA: National Leadership Training Pro-

gram in the Area of the Deaf, San Fernando Valley State College (now California State University, Northridge), 1970.

Johnson, M. et al., eds. *Proceedings of the Third Biennial Registry of Interpreters for the Deaf, Inc. National Workshop/ Convention* (Seattle, 1974). Seattle: Washington State Registry of Interpreters for the Deaf, 1974.

Jones, Michael and Quigley, Stephen. "Selection, Evaluation and Classification of Interpreters." *Journal of Rehabilitation of the Deaf* 8:1:79–84.

Jones, Ray L., Project Director. *A Community Program for Identification, Training and Utilization of Interpreting Services for Deaf Persons; Materials Prepared for a Workshop to Activate Interpreting Services for the Deaf, San Francisco, 1966.* National Leadership Training Program in the Area of the Deaf, San Fernando Valley State College (now California State University Northridge).

Jordan, I. King; Gustason, Gerilee; and Rosen, Roslyn. "An Update on Communication Trends at Programs for the Deaf." *American Annals of the Deaf* 124:350–357.

Kannapell, Barbara M.; Hamilton, Lillian B., and Bornstein Harry. *Signs for Instructional Purposes.* Washington, DC: Gallaudet College Press, 1969.

Keller, Maree Jo. *Survey: Understanding the Interpreter.* Northridge, CA: California State University, Northridge, 1972.

Kirchner, Carl J. ed., Professional or Amateur; Southern California Registry of Interpreters for the Deaf, Workshop #1—Proceedings, 1969, Northridge, CA: San Fernando Valley State College (now California State University, Northridge).

Kirchner, Carl J. ed., *Project Learn: Southern California Registry of Interpreters for the Deaf, Workshop #2—Proceedings.* Northridge, CA: San Fernando Valley State College (now California State University, Northridge), 1970.

Klima, Edward and Bellugi, Ursula. *The Signs of Language.* Cambridge, MA: Harvard University Press, 1979.

LeBuffe, James, eds. *Sterck, Ogletown, Smith—Program "Mainstream."* Newark: DE: Newark School District, 1975.

Legal Seminar. Dunedin, FL: Florida Registry of Interpreters for the Deaf, 1972.

Levine, Edna. *Interpreting for the Deaf: Analysing a New Profession* (unpublished paper), 1972.

Levine, Edna and Flynn, John. "Analysis of Contributing Characteristics to Effective Interpretation for the Deaf." *Proceedings, 79th Annual Convention* (American Psychological Association). Washington, DC: American Psychological Association, 1971).

Levine, Edna and Flynn, John. *Materials Associated with Levine-Flynn Research* (unpublished materials). 1970.

Lloyd, Glenn. "Problems Associated with Interpreting for the Deaf Person in Large groups" in G. Lloyd, ed. *Guidelines for Effective Participation of Deaf Persons in Professional Meetings.* Washington, DC: Department of Health, Education and Welfare 1971, 107–111.

Madsen, Willard J. *Conversational Sign Language II.* Gallaudet College, Washington, D.C., 1972.

Morgan, Susan. "Interpreting as an Interpreter Sees It." *Journal of Rehabilitation of the Deaf* 7:3:28–32.

Murphy, Harry, ed. *Educational Interpreting.* Southern California Registry of Interpreters for the Deaf.

Murphy, Harry. *Perceptions of Deaf Persons and Interpreters of the Deaf of an "Ideal" Interpreter* (paper presented at Registry of Interpreters for the Deaf convention, Rochester, NY, 1978).

Murphy, Harry. "Research in Sign Language Interpreting at CSUN" in D. Gerver and H. W. Sinaiko, eds. *Language Interpretation and Communication.* New York, NY: Plenum Press, 1978.

Murphy, Harry, ed. *Selected Readings in the Integration of Deaf Students at CSUN.* Northridge: California State University, Northridge, National Center on Deafness Publication Series, 1976.

Myers, Lowell J. *How Does the Interpreter Get Paid in a Court Case Involving a Deaf Person?* Chicago, 1971.

Myers, Lowell J. *How to Get a New State Law for Court Interpreters for the Deaf.* Chicago, 1971.

Myers, Lowell J. *How to Write a Model Law for Interpreters for the Deaf.* Chicago, IL: 1969.

Neesam, Ralph. "Rating Forms and Check Lists for Interpreters." *Journal of Rehabilitation of the Deaf* 2:1:19–28.

Neesam, Ralph. "The Registry of Interpreters for the Deaf" in T. J. O'Rourke, ed. *Psycholinguistics and Total Communica-*

tion: The State of the Art. Washington, DC: *American Annals of the Deaf,* 1972.

Northcott, Winifred. "Letter to the Editor." *American Annals of the Deaf* 124:4.

Northcott, Winifred. "The Oral Interpreter: A Necessary Support Specialist for the Hearing Impaired." *Volta Review* 79:136–145.

Nowell, Richard and Stuckless, E. Ross. "An Interpreter Training Program." *Journal of Rehabilitation of the Deaf* 7:3:69–76.

O'Rourke, Terrence J. *A Basic Course in Manual Communication,* rev. ed., Silver Spring, MD: National Association of the Deaf, 1973.

Palmer, Jim, ed. *Proceedings of the Second National Workshop/ Convention of the Registry of Interpreters for the Deaf, 1972.* Northridge, CA: Joyce Publications, 1974.

Pernick, Joseph. *Handbook for "Interpreting in the Legal Setting" Workshop.* Northridge, CA: California State University, Northridge, 1973.

Pimentel, Albert, "Interpreting Services for Deaf People." *Journal of Rehabilitation of the Deaf* 3:1:112–120.

Pimental, Albert. *National Certification of Interpreters: A Manual for Evaluators.* Washington, DC: Registry of Interpreters for the Deaf, 1972.

Pricket, Bill and Rash, Norman. "Use of Interpreters in the Vocational Rehabilitation Process." *Journal of Rehabilitation of the Deaf* 9:4:11–15.

Purvis, J. Rox. *Some Attitudes and Characteristics of Persons Attending the Second Southern California Registry of Interpreters for the Deaf Workshop.* Northridge, CA: National Leadership Training Program in the Area of the Deaf, San Fernando Valley State College (now California State University, Northridge), 1970.

Quigley, Stephen, ed. Interpreting for Deaf People. Washington, DC: Department of Health, Education, and Welfare, 1965.

Quigley, Stephen; Brasel, Barbara B.; and Wilbur, Ronnie. "A Survey of Interpreters for Deaf People in the State of Illinois." *Journal of Rehabilitation of the Deaf* 6:1:7–11.

Registry of Interpreters for the Deaf. "Interprenews." *The Deaf American,* 1972 to 1977.

Registry of Interpreters for the Deaf. *Introduction to Interpreting*. Silver Spring, MD: Registry of Interpreters for the Deaf, 1980.

Registry of Interpreters for the Deaf. *Principles, Guidelines and Standards Proposed for R.I.D., Inc. Accreditation of Interpreter Training Programs*. Washington, DC: Registry of Interpreters for the Deaf, 1978.

Registry of Interpreters for the Deaf National Certification Board. *Questions, Answers, and Guidelines for R.I.D. Evaluations*. Silver Spring, MD: Registry of Interpreters for the Deaf, 1973.

Reynolds, Maynard and Birch, Jack. *Teaching Exceptional Children in All America's Schools*. Reston, VA: The Council for Exceptional Children, 1977.

Riekehof, Lottie. "Factors Related to Interpreter Proficiency" in Williams, Clarence, ed. *Language and Communication Research Problems*. Washington, DC: Gallaudet College Press, 1976.

Riekehof, Lottie. "Interpreter Training at Gallaudet College." *Journal of Rehabilitation of the Deaf* 7:3:47–52.

Riekehof, Lottie. *The Joy of Signing*. Springfield, MO: Gospel Publishing House, 1978.

Riekehof, Lottie. *Talk to the Deaf; A Manual of Approximately 1,000 Signs Used by the Deaf of North America,* Springfield, MO: Gospel Publishing House, 1963.

Rosen, Roslyn. "Deafness and Implications for Mainstreaming" in *PL 94–142 and Deaf Children* (special issue of the Gallaudet Alumni Newsletter). Washington, DC: Gallaudet College, 1977.

Rudser, Steve; Witter, Anna; and Gillies, Katharine. *NTID Interpreting Services "State of the Art."* Rochester, NY: National Technical Institute for the Deaf, 1978.

Rudy, Les. H. *A Survey of Attending Behaviors of Deaf Graduate Students to Interpreters*. Northridge, CA: National Leadership Training Program in the Area of the Deaf, California State University, Northridge, 1973.

San Fernando Valley State College. A Community Program for Identification, Training and Utilization of Interpreting Services for Deaf Persons. Northridge, CA: San Fernando Valley State College (now California State University, Northridge),

National Leadership Training Program in the Area of the Deaf, 1966.

San Fernando Valley State College. *Proceedings of a Conference for Teachers and Interpreters in Adult Education Programs for the Deaf.* Northridge, CA: San Fernando Valley State College (now California State University, Northridge), 1966.

Sanderson, Robert G. "Interpreting as the Deaf See It," *Rehabilitation Record,* January-February 1967, p. 17–19.

Schein, Jerome. "Personality Characteristics Associated with Interpeter Proficiency." *Journal of Rehabilitation of the Deaf* 7:33:33–34.

Schlesinger, Hilde and Meadow, Kathryn. "Interpreting for Deaf Persons: A Contribution to Mental Health." The Deaf American 20:11:5–8.

Smith, Jess., ed. *Workshop on Interpreting for the Deaf.* Muncie, IN: Ball State Teachers College, 1964.

Smith, Jess., ed. *Workshop to Activate Interpreting Services for the Deaf* (San Francisco, CA: 1966).

Smith, T. Michael et al. *Considerations in the Design and Development of Interpreter Education Programs* (Technical Report #1). Rochester, NY: National Technical Institute for the Deaf, Interpreter Education Program, 1978.

Smith, T. Michael and Finch, Karen. *Teaching Voice (Reverse) Interpreting* (Technical Report #4). Rochester, NY: National Technical Institute for the Deaf, Interpreter Education Program, 1978.

Smith, T. Michael and Gorelick, Aaron. *The Admissions Process of the Basic Interpreter Training Program: A Formative Evaluation* (Technical Report #3). Rochester, NY: National Technical Institute for the Deaf, Interpreter Education Program.

Smith, Theresa. *Guidelines for Working/Playing with Deaf-Blind People* (unpublished paper). 1977.

Southern California Registry of Interpreters for the Deaf. *Professional or Amateur,* Northridge, CA: Southern California Registry of Interpreters for the Deaf, 1969.

Southern California Registry of Interpreters for the Deaf. *Project Learn.* Northridge, CA: Southern California Registry of Interpreters for the Deaf, 1970.

Sternberg, Martin. "Brief, Intensive Training to Develop Interpreters." *Journal of Rehabilitation of the Deaf* 7:3:63–69.

Sternberg, Martin; Tipton, Carol; and Schein, Jerome. *Curriculum Guide for Interpreter Training*. New York, NY: New York University, Deafness Research and Training Center, 1973.

Stokoe, William C.; Croneberg, Carl G.; Casterline, Dorothy C. *A Dictionary of American Sign Language on Linguistic Principles*. Washington, DC: Gallaudet College Press, 1976.

Stokoe, William C. "Sign Language Structure: An Outline of the Visual Communication Systems of the American Deaf." *Studies in Linguistics. Occasional Papers, 8*. Buffalo, NY: University of Buffalo, Department of Anthroplogy and Linguistics, 1960.

Straub, Edward. "Interpreting for the Deaf in a Psychiatric Setting." *Journal of Rehabilitation* 10:2:15–21.

Stuckless, E. R. and Enders, M. *A Study of Selected Support Services for Post-secondary Deaf Students in Regular Classes* (working paper). Rochester, NY: National Technical Institute for the Deaf, 1971.

Taylor, Lucille, ed. *Proceedings of a Follow-up Workshop on Interpreting for the Deaf*. Washington: DC: Department of Health, Education, and Welfare, 1965.

Tipton, Carol. "Interpreting Ethics." *Journal of Rehabilitation of the Deaf* 7:4:10–17.

Titus, James. *The Comparative Effectiveness of Presenting Spoken Information to Postsecondary Oral Deaf Students Through a Live Speaker, an Oral Interpreter, and an Interpreter Using Signed English* (unpublished doctoral dissertation). Pittsburgh, PA: University of Pittsburgh, 1978.

Tweney, Ryan. "Sign Language and Psycholinguistic Process: Fact, Hypotheses, and Implications for Interpretation." In D. Gerver and H. W. Sinaiko, eds. *Language Interpretation and Communication*. New York, NY: Plenum Press, 1978.

Tweney, Ryan and Hoemann, Harry. "Translation and Sign Languages" in R. Brislin, ed. *Translation: Applications and Research*. New York, NY: Gardner Press, 1976.

Utah State Board of Education. *Report on a Workshop for Training Interpreters for the Deaf*. Salt Lake City, UT: Utah State Board of Education, 1972.

Vernon, McCay and Coley, Joan. "Violation of Constitutional Rights: The Language Impaired Person and the Miranda Warnings." *Journal of Rehabilitation of the Deaf* 11:4:1–7.

Vernon, McCay and Prickett, Hugh, Jr. "Mainstreaming: Issues and Model Plan." *Audiology and Hearing Education* 2:2:5–9.

Vidrine, Jacqueline A. *A Historical Study of the Neo-Professional Organization Registry of Interpreters for the Deaf, Inc.* (1964–1978) (unpublished doctoral dissertation). New Orleans, LA: Tulane University, 1979.

Vidrine, Jacqueline. Interpreter Training Programs. New Orleans, LA: Delgado College.

Wampler, Dennis. *Linguistics of Visual English, Booklets 1–3,* Santa Rosa, CA: 1971.

Washington State School for the Deaf. *An Introduction to Manual English,* Vancouver, WA: Washington State School for the Deaf, 1972.

Watson, David. *Talk With Your Hands,* Vol. I, II. Silver Spring, MD: National Association of the Deaf, 1972.

White, Ralph. *A Basic Glossary of Legal Terms.* Northridge, CA: National Leadership Training Program in the Area of the Deaf, San Fernando Valley State College (now California State University, Northridge), 1966.

Witter, Anna. *Oral Interpreter Certification* (unpublished paper). Rochester, NY: National Technical Institute for the Deaf, 1979.

Witter, Anna, et al. *Certification of Oral Interpreters* (unpublished paper). Rochester, NY: National Technical Institute for the Deaf, 1979.

Woodward, James. "Sex is Definitely a Problem: Interpreters' Knowledge of Signs for Sexual Behavior." *Sign Language Studies* 14:73–77.

Woodward, James. *Signs of Drug Use.* Silver Spring, MD: T. J. Publishers, 1980.

Woodward, James. *Signs of Sexual Behavior.* Silver Spring, MD: T. J. Publishers, 1979.

Woodward, James. "Some Observations on Sociolinguistic Variation and American Sign Language." *Kansas Journal of Sociology* 9:2:191–199.

Yoken, Carol, ed. *Interpreter Training: The State of the Art.* Washington, DC: The National Academy of Gallaudet College, 1980.

Youngs, Joseph, Jr. "Interpreting for Deaf Clients." *Journal of Rehabilitation of the Deaf* 1:1:49–55.

About The Author

SHARON NEUMANN SOLOW began interpreting professionally while still in High School, interpreting in a doctoral program at the University of Arizona. After graduation, she interpreted at NTID in Rochester, New York during its first year of
operation. Next she moved to California State University,
Northridge, where she interpreted part-time and received her
B.A. in English. She spent the following year in San Diego working and studying with Dr. Ursula Bellugi at the Salk Institute
researching ASL. After another year back at CSUN as Lead
Interpreter and interpreter trainer, Sharon moved to Seattle.
There she taught in the Interpreter Training Program at Seattle
Community College and received her M.A. in Adult Education
from Seattle University. Now she is back in Northridge teaching, after a year as Faculty Liaison for the National Center on
Deafness. She teaches a song sign class, interpreting and ASL,
and trains and evaluates interpreters. Ms. Neumann Solow has
coordinated the training of legal interpreters for the state of
California, and holds a Comprehensive Skills Certificate (CSC)
and a Specialist Certificate: Legal (SC:L). She has extensive
experience in many aspects of Sign Language interpreting and
in interpreter and Sign Language training. She also holds a Sign
Instructor Guidance Network's Comprehensive Permanent Certificate. She has travelled throughout the United States serving
as interpreter, performer, trainer and consultant. Sharon is the
female lead in the Electric Sign Company, a song signing duo.
She and her husband, Larry, have an NBC television series
teaching Sign Language. Ms. Neumann Solow has appeared in a
number of other television performances as an interpreter, song
signer and host. Sharon and Larry's darling daughter, Megan
was born into their lives June 21, 1979 and brings them great
joy.

NATIONAL ASSOCIATION OF THE DEAF

The Manual Alphabet
(as seen by the receiver)

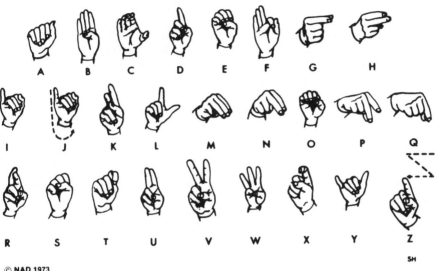

A B C D E F G H

I J K L M N O P Q

R S T U V W X Y Z

SH

© NAD 1973

DID YOU KNOW YOUR BOOK PURCHASES CAN HELP SUPPORT THE OLDEST AND LARGEST CONSUMER ORGANIZATION OF HANDICAPPED PEOPLE IN THE UNITED STATES—THE NATIONAL ASSOCIATION OF THE DEAF?

The National Association of the Deaf is a private, nonprofit association operating independently of federal and state governments. It is supported by a dedicated membership and by others interested in the aims of the NAD. You can help support this organization through your purchases of books and films. The revenue earned from book sales makes it possible for us to provide the services and programs of this organization.

As a leading publisher in the area of deafness and sign language, the NAD prepares a Catalog of Publications twice yearly. It is filled with materials about deafness—sign language books, films, videotapes, gift items, etc. It contains items not only published by the NAD but those items sold by other publishers as well. In this way we can offer a wide variety of materials all available from one place. We offer excellent service, shipping all orders via United Parcel Service. As with all reputable mail order companies, your satisfaction is guaranteed and we will cheerfully refund your money if you are not satisfied with our materials.

If you would like to receive a FREE copy of our Catalog of Publications, please fill in the postage paid card below and we will ship one to you immediately. If you have a friend who might be interested in receiving our catalog, please send us his/her name as well.

PLEASE SEND MY FREE CATALOG TO: | PLEASE SEND A CATALOG TO MY FRIEND:

Name

Address

City   State   Zip Code

Name

Address

City   State   Zip Code

_____ PLEASE ADD MY NAME TO YOUR MAILING LIST